Surprised in Translation

Surprised in Translation

Mary Ann Caws

The University of Chicago Press
Chicago & London

Mary Ann Caws is Distinguished Professor of English, French, and Comparative Literature at the Graduate Center of the City University of New York and an *officier* of the Palmes Académiques. Among her many publications are, most recently, *Pablo Picasso, Surrealism, Surrealist Poets and Painters, To the Boathouse: A Memoir*, and *Surrealist Love Poems*, the latter published by the University of Chicago Press.

The University of Chicago Press, Chicago 60637
The University of Chicago Press, Ltd., London
© 2006 by Mary Ann Caws
All rights reserved. Published 2006
Printed in the United States of America

15 14 13 12 11 10 09 08 07 06   1 2 3 4 5

ISBN-13: 978-0-226-09873-9 (cloth)
ISBN-10: 0-226-09873-7 (cloth)

Library of Congress Cataloging-in-Publication Data
Caws, Mary Ann.
    Surprised in translation / Mary Ann Caws.
        p. cm.
    Includes bibliographical references and index.
    ISBN 0-226-09873-7 (alk. paper)
    1. French poetry—Translations into English—History and criticism. I. Title.
PQ143.E5C39 2006
428'.0241—dc22

                                                            2006000831

Contents

Preface: A Note on Surprise

THE ORIGIN OF this book was surprise. The translations I find most appealing have something odd about them. Most of the translations discussed here struck me with a jolt: that energizing shock gave birth to the chapters, one by one. Sometimes it was occasioned by the elimination of various passages in the original, as if poetic license included the permission to suppress—this is true of the chapters on Mallarmé (his translations of Tennyson), Pound (his translations of Rimbaud and Arnaut Daniel), and Woolf (her translations by Clara Malraux); sometimes by the opposite, the translation yielding a longer form than the original (Bonnefoy's renderings of Shakespeare, Keats, and Yeats); and sometimes by a sort of swerve in the meaning, true of many of these translations, including Beckett's of his own texts and of others. Each of these surprises could be justified and, just as easily, attacked. What has interested me is the frequency of the unexpected, the unmimetic, and how very well that works.

None of the poets translating and translated in these pages deal in the predictable. Translate, says Yves Bonnefoy, poets who are close to you; I have endeavored to do that, have surrounded the translations with context wherever I could do so—including the anecdotal, often the clue to the tone of text and translation—and have included remarks on my own translations and retranslations or rereadings, which are to me the heart of the translating endeavor.

Acknowledgments

FIRST OF ALL, for all the friends and listeners who put up with my incessant going on about Alex the gray parrot, I am most grateful: among so many others, these include Boyce Bennett, Carolyn Gill, Mette and Christopher MacRae, Don and Vera Murray, Irene Pepperberg, Christopher Prendergast, Martin and Mary Sixsmith, Malcolm and Janet Swan, and Josh Wilner. For a place to think about translation and other endeavors, I am thankful for the Rockefeller Foundation's Villa Serbelloni at Bellagio. For the unpublished letters of Vanessa Bell and Roger Fry, I want to thank the Archives of Tate Britain, London, and the archivists for their invaluable help; for the unpublished letter from Virginia Woolf to Charles Mauron, I want to thank Alice Mauron. For various collaborative efforts, in thinking about the so-vexed topic of translation and in translating this and that, I want to thank Nicole Brossard, Jean-Pierre Cauvin, Hilary Caws-Elwitt, Matthew Caws, Peter Caws, Linda and Arthur Collins, Serge Gavronsky, Marilyn Hacker, Geoffrey Harris, James Lawler, Rosemary Lloyd, Sara Mugridge, Grace Schulman, Martin Sorrell, and Patricia Terry. For their enthusiastic support of various publishing endeavors related to this one, I want to thank Olivier Brossard—whose contact with the French Cultural Services was invaluable—John Kulka of Yale University Press, Randy Petilos of the University of Chicago Press, Declan Spring of New Directions, as well as Jill Anderson, Marie-Claude Char, Gerhard Joseph, Mary

Maxwell, John Naughton, Lois Oppenheim, Jean-Michel Rabaté, and Julian Wolfreys. For her sustained enthusiasm, thanks to my agent, Katherine Fausset. For superb editing, thanks to Erin DeWitt. For his support over the years and his generous translator's spirit, I want to thank Yves Bonnefoy, who taught me to translate only poets I love. Thank you.

I would like to thank the publishers for permission to reprint the following entire poems or translations thereof. In chapter 3: Pierre Reverdy's "Quand on n'est pas de ce monde" and my translation, "When One Is Not of This World," in Pierre Reverdy's *Selected Poems*, trans. John Ashbery, Mary Ann Caws, and Patricia Terry (Winston-Salem, NC: Wake Forest University Press, 1991); Roger Shattuck's translation of Guillaume Apollinaire's "Adieu," "I picked this fragile sprig of heather," in *Selected Writings of Guillaume Apollinaire*, trans. Roger Shattuck (New York: New Directions, 1971), © Roger Shattuck; used by permission of New Directions.

In chapter 4: Roger Fry's translation of Stéphane Mallarmé's "Apparition" and my translation of Mallarmé's "Le Pitre châtié"/"The Chastised Clown," in *Selected Poetry and Prose*, by Stéphane Mallarmé, © 1982 by Mary Ann Caws, reprinted by permission of New Directions Publishing Corp.

In chapter 6: Ezra Pound's translation of the Marquise de Boufflers's "Air: Sentir avec ardeur"; of Arnaut Daniel's "Chansson Doil"; and of Arthur Rimbaud's "Vénus anadyomène," "Première soirée," "Chercheuses de poux," and "Au Cabaret-Vert"—all in *The Translations of Ezra Pound*, © 1963 by Ezra Pound, reprinted with permission of New Directions Publishing Corp.

In chapter 7: Samuel Beckett's translations of Sébastien Chamfort's "Quand on soutient que les gens"; of his own "Elles viennent," "Eneug II," and "Malacoda"; of Paul Éluard's "L'univers-solitude," "Scène," and "Confections"; of Arthur Rimbaud's "Le bateau ivre"; and of Guillaume Apollinaire's "Zone," in *Collected Poems by English and French*, by Samuel Beckett, © 1977 by Samuel Beckett; used by permission of Grove/Atlantic, Inc. Also Beckett's translation of René Char's "Courbet: *Les Casseurs de cailloux*," in *Dehors la nuit est gouvernée*, in *Oeuvres complètes*, © Éditions Gallimard, Paris, 1983.

In chapter 8: Yves Bonnefoy's translation of Shakespeare's sonnets 73, 129, 146, in "Douze sonnets de Shakespeare," *Nu(e)*, no. 25, special issue "Michel Collet" (March 2003): 95–106. Sonnets 73 and

129 in "La traduction des sonnets de Shakespeare," in *Shakespeare et la France*, Société française Shakespeare, Actes du Congrès de 2000. Textes réunis et présentés par Patricia Dorval. Publiés sous la direction de Jean-Marie Maguin (Paris: Société française Shakespeare, 2001), p. 62 (sonnet 129); p. 65 (sonnet 73); see also William Shakespeare, *Les Poèmes de Shakespeare, précédé de traduire en vers ou en prose*, trans. Yves Bonnefoy (Paris: Mercure de France, 1993). Courtesy of Yves Bonnefoy. Passages from Pierre-Jean Jouve's translations in *Shakespeare. Sonnets* (Paris: *Poésie* Gallimard, 1969).

In the final chapter, "Coda": Thanks to Martin Sorrell for his translation of Robert Desnos's "Hour farther."

I also thank the following journals for their permission to reprint the following pieces or adaptations thereof: portions of chapter 4 originally appeared as "Translation and the Art of Friendship, Signed Mallarmé and Whistler," *Yearbook of Comparative and General Literature*, no. 42 (1994); "Bloomsbury's Mallarmé," in *Australian Divagations: Mallarmé and the Twentieth Century*, ed. Jill Anderson (New York: Peter Lang, 2002); and "Naming and Not Naming: Tennyson and Mallarmé," *Victorian Poetry* 43 (2005), the portion of the article that I wrote with my coauthor, Gerhard Joseph. Portions of chapter 5 originally appeared as "Taking Our Time with Things: Virginia Woolf's Object Lessons," in *Virginia Woolf Bulletin* (Bordeaux, France, 1999); and "Virginia Woolf in French Translation," in *The European Reception of Virginia Woolf*, ed. Mary Ann Caws and Nicola Luckhurst (New York: Continuum, 2002). Chapter 6 originally appeared as "Ezra Pound: Writer as Translator," in a special issue edited by Hélène Aji titled "Ezra Pound dans le vortex de la traduction," for *Annales du Monde Anglophone* 16 (Paris: L'Harmattan, 2002). Chapter 7 originally appeared as "Samuel Beckett Translating," in *Samuel Beckett Today/Aujourd'hui*, vol. 8 (Amsterdam: Rodopi, 1999). And a portion of chapter 8 first appeared as "Bonnefoy Translates Yeats," *Dalhousie French Studies* 60 (Fall 2002).

All unattributed translations throughout are my own.

1. The Salmon and Some Parrots

TWO SUMMERS AGO, it was. Things were swaying about me, at the house of my friends, down the hill in the tiny perched village in Provence where I live my summers, and I had to hold on to the side of the dark green door. In nearby Carpentras, the vertigo expert said he would try something I thought he called "la manoeuvre saumon," or the "salmon maneuver." Fine, I said, and was astonished to find myself thrown suddenly on my side and with a great force upon the examining table. It was, he said, to readjust the little hairs in the inner ear. So "salmon" and "hearing" seemed to me intimately connected.

Only it was about mishearing and misinterpretation. As I found out recently from the *Herald-Tribune*, that particular maneuver—which "requires the patient's head and body to be tilted, turned and swung," directing the little particles deranging the hair cell receptors to go back to their place—was invented by a Dr. Sémont. So "Sémont" was my "salmon," and the ear is plainly unreliable.

Clearly, the salmon case with its (my) nonexactness would be the opposite of what happens in the case of the parrot, wouldn't it? We think of parrots as perfect repeaters of what they hear: they don't have hearing troubles or get dizzy from them. In Julian Barnes's brilliant story *Flaubert's Parrot*, the chase for the "authentic" parrot who would have served the author for his model of the giant parakeet in "Félicité" (one of his stories in *Trois contes*) results in total confusion about which might be the genuine parrot. Geoffrey Braithwaite, the heavily un-ironic academic who narrates the tale, finds in the Hôtel-Dieu of Rouen a bright green stuffed bird labeled: "*Psittacus:* Parrot borrowed by G. Flaubert from the Museum of Rouen and placed on his work-table during the writing of *Un coeur simple*, where it is called Loulou, the parrot of Félicité, the principal character in the tale" (Barnes 16). But in Flaubert's residence at Croisset, he finds another parrot, deemed "less authentic than the first" (21), having a more benign air. Finally, he ends up confronting the notion of not two or just three but fifty or so parrots, in a splendid mockery of the ideas of repetition and exactitude, exemplifying "the Flaubertian grotesque" (17).

Among the specialists in parrot culture, Bruce Thomas Boehrer is notable as the author of *Parrot Culture*, which examines the bird's history, from Alexander the Great, who imported the parrot into India, to today. He also discusses private parrot passions, including that for the Alexandrine parakeet and his own bird. If the famous Alex of my favorite story has his own heritage transcribed in the repetition of his name, the whole idea of parroting in art and text has numerous recounters, and the bird reappears everywhere, from Shakespeare and John Skelton's "Speke, Parrot" of 1525, to Edgar Allan Poe. Think of Robert Louis Stevenson's *Treasure Island*, Kate Chopin's "The Awakening," Princess Marthe Bibesco's *Green Parrot*, Flaubert and Barnes's *Flaubert's Parrot*; of Colette, Woolf, Gabriel García Márquez, and Margaret Atwood's *Oryx and Crake*; and the artists Courbet, Manet, Renoir, Miró, Cornell, Max Beckmann, and Frida Kahlo; and then the various White House parrots, including those of Martha Washington, Dolly Madison, Grace Coolidge, and the Roosevelts; and the celebrated ex-parrot of *Monty Python's Flying Circus*, to say nothing of the wild parrots of Brooklyn, who have inspired a 2006 "Urban Parrots" calendar. "Let them guide your flight," reads the text.

In Jonathan Safran Foer's piece for *Conjunctions*, called "Finitude: Selections from the Permanent Collection," we find the following wall tag:

Shakespeare's Parrot's Parrot's Parrot's Parrot's Parrot's Parrot's Parrot's Parrot's Parrot's Parrot's Parrot. 1942–? Striped West Indian Parrot, approx. 14 x 5 in. Museum purchase.

Little is known of the man who is widely considered the greatest writer in history. The best insight into who he was may lie in the parrot perched before you, a tenth-generation descendant of the parrot given to Shakespeare in 1610 as a gift by his friend and fellow poet Michael Drayton. The Bard was exceedingly fond of the bird, and would speak to her as one might write in a journal—to chronicle, reflect and confess. When he died of fever six years later, Anne Hathaway kept the parrot, and introduced into its cage a younger parrot, to learn what the older could teach it. She never spoke to either of them, and forbade guests from speaking in their presence. A line of Shakespeare's parrots was raised in the painstaking silence of her love, and when she died, our reverence. And so we ask you not to speak while in this sound-proof room, but only to listen. We ask you not to compromise the very weakening but direct line from this parrot to Shakespeare. And when it begs you, "Talk to me," as it has the habit of doing, we ask you not to give it the company of your voice— it is not the parrot, remember, who begs to be talked to, and while Shakespeare may reach us through the parrot, it will never work in the other direction. (73)

Contemporary critics are haunted by the notion of the parrot; witness the controversy over Alex, the African gray, whose skills at age twenty-three are lauded by Irene Pepperberg, his owner and trainer, in her book *The Alex Studies*. Do parrots think or just repeat? What about their cognitive processes? My own parroting passion came about first through reading, in Hillel Schwartz's *Culture of the Copy*, another story about the very smart Alex, which he reports having taken from a publication by Dr. Pepperberg. (That the story isn't entirely veridical I didn't find out until later, when I consulted Irene Pepperberg, a fact that perfectly illustrates the issues of translation, retranslation, and retelling.) Anyway, here is the story, as Schwartz tells it.

In Alex's cage there was a mirror, toward which he would turn, saying, "I am going to go away" (Schwartz 152). One day, looking in his mirror, he asked his trainer, out of the blue, it seems, "What color?" Said the trainer: "That's gray. You are a gray parrot." Alex said to the mirror or to himself in it, "Gray parrot" (Schwartz 152). This, on my first reading, seemed to me already a step beyond simple repetition, something about identity seeking and curiosity. Instead of simply repeating something, the parrot was initiating a discussion with his mirror image, albeit defined by someone else's answer, by some authoritative outsider. He was accepting the definition, and upon reflection, as it were, he might have been trying to persuade himself to accept it.

If I continue to feel so strongly about that story, it is because of the play on and beyond the mimetic by its primary enactor, as we have been accustomed to thinking of parroting as the mimetic moment par excellence. This parrot manages to make the question of identity interesting, both his own and his opposite in my own mythmaking, in the mistaken identity of the salmon that never existed except in my earshot. This would be the perfect salmon maneuver, finding something through a mistake or long shot, and finding it all the more convincing through this slippage.

Irene Pepperberg's own published recountings of her training of Alex and of their relationship added other angles to the story: how Alex could recognize colors like orange and blue, as well as shapes like triangles and squares; how he demanded his rewards; what their relationship was like. But it was still the question Alex asked ("What color?") and his repetition of his identity to himself and to his mirror ("Gray parrot") that enticed me. I began to repeat this story often, in many sorts of diverse contexts, and the reactions were just as diverse. Writing a piece on some of the excitement these days on the relation between art and text, "Looking: Literature's Other," I ended it on my Alex story. An obsessive reaction, clearly: at moments I thought perhaps it had something to do with Wittgenstein's use of language and discussions of cognition—but what? It was quite as if an event had transpired, an anecdote had been told, in some language that I could not or could no longer translate. I kept trying to put together this story of mistaken identity, in the case of the salmon, and found identity, in the case of Alex the African gray parrot, the unchallenged hero of my tale.

A year later, in February 2005, the tale of Dr. Pepperberg and Alex develops, filled in by a third recounter, now with a surprise. In Temple Grandin's *Animals in Translation: Using the Mysteries of Autism to Decode Animal Behavior*, Alex, now twenty-five, reappears, in a differently angled telling of his tale, in relation to the autistic personality. It turns out that Dr. Pepperberg had asked Alex questions such as "What color?" and "What shape?"—and so the purport and the shape of the question were familiar to him. Grandin's phrasing of the event, and her marveling at it, stresses the moment when Alex started asking questions on his own—unusual in animals and in autistic humans:

> One day he looked at his reflection in the mirror and asked Dr. Pepperberg, "What color?"
> After he'd asked about his own color six different times, and heard answers like "That's gray; you're a gray parrot" six different times, he knew gray as a category. From then on he could tell his trainer whether or not any object she showed him was gray. (251–52)

Here is what Grandin marvels at: Alex's recognition of abstract categories, such as "blueness," "redness," "squareness," and so on, in previously unexperienced situations, an ability she links to reclassification. Whereas the autistic and—in general— the animal personality focus on the concrete and the classification, here Alex is into abstract thinking and reclassifying, jumping orders of things. In her book *Through Our Eyes Only?* Marian Stamp Dawkins gives, says Grandin, the definition of true cognition as the ability to solve a problem under novel conditions (Grandin 243). So Alex was capable of cognition.

The other point about Alex's training was that, as opposed to behavioral modeling (reward and punishment), Pepperberg used "social modeling": with Alex watching, she would show her assistant a lovely blue crunchy piece of bark—something Alex would dearly love to get his beak on—and then ask, "What color?" When the assistant answered correctly, then he could play with the bark (Grandin 250).

But the totally surprising element is this: One day, at the media lab, there was a long question-and-answer period between Dr. Pepperberg and Alex, in front of visiting colleagues, about the color of some plastic refrigerator letters and the sounds associated with them. She had not yet given Alex the nut he was used to receiving after correctly answering. Dr. Pepperberg would ask, "Alex, what sound is blue?" and he would make the sound "Ssss" and for the sound of green, he would say, "Sssh." On each occasion he followed his answer with "Want a nut." And, as Dr. Pepperberg recently told me, she was trying to get in as much as she could with the few minutes she had with the visitors and ignored his request, telling him to wait. But then he lost his patience, and said Dr. Pepperberg, as quoted by Temple Grandin: "Alex gets very slitty-eyed and he looks at me and states, 'Want a nut. Nnn, uh, tuh.'" Writes Temple Grandin: *"Alex had spelled 'nut'"* (282). He was way ahead of the trainers, who had been working with him for twenty years without knowing he could spell. They did not know, despite being experts in animal cognition, how to *perceive*.

So I had to review my heretofore readings of Alex and his own parroting experience on three separate occasions, relatively far apart in time, to get my own animal-in-translation experience in shape. Readjustment, rereading, and—sometimes—rewriting are part of what translation has been about for me. Really, translation is about all of this: mishearing and parroting correctly, making jumps in orders and reclassifying, perceiving in concrete and abstract terms, allowing and creating the slippages and reshapings that will best work. Finally—most crucially—it may be about rethinking in order to retranslate, with some degree of surprise. Perhaps it is about being, as in a recent group of experiments reported in the *New York Times*, not timid birds but bold ones. Here's to the bold birds.

II. *Translating Together*

AMONG THE MANY collaborative translations I have been involved in—all of them instructive and few of them, I like to hope, disastrous—one of the most appropriate and most amusing was the joint work that Patricia Terry and I plunged ourselves into when we tackled part of Stéphane Mallarmé's journal *La Dernière Mode* for my 2001 edition of *Mallarmé in Prose*. We had previously translated together such poets as André Breton, René Char, Victor Hugo, Louise Labé, Valéry Larbaud, Pierre Reverdy, Victor Segalen, Philippe Soupault, and Paul Valéry, as well as a few poems by the Master himself.

What seemed so appropriate this time about the idea of a collaborative translation was tackling the various voices assumed by Mallarmé for this short-lived journal, the great majority of articles written by himself, in the guise of Mademoiselle X, Mademoiselle Satin, Marguerite de Ponty, Brébant's Chef de Bouche, Olympia la négresse, and a bunch of readers from Alsace and elsewhere. In these various voices, we discussed costumes and food and travels and labored over the varieties of cold cream and bustles endlessly. Not one moment was dull.

How could we possibly approximate the many voices of these personae? Marguerite de Ponty's smarmy camaraderie: "There is, in jewelry, something permanent—don't you agree? . . . Let's admire the Jewel itself. Where shall we find it?" (79) and her simpering:

"As for lace, we prefer it to be very precious, made by the hands of the fairies themselves, in their total ignorance of mediocrity" (81). A reader from Alsace enthuses about "the curls of Baby Jesus" atop the Christmas tree. And so on: we were finally so taken by our endeavor that we wanted to imitate it—fortunately, that project came to naught.

When you know each other's translating mind well enough, you can see what is coming to something and what isn't: that is the truest sense of the collaborative work.

III. *Greeting, Slippage, and Shaping*

AS SOMEONE SPECIFICALLY interested in the translation of poetry, of the free verse variety, I will come down squarely on the side of occasional long shots, slippages into the non-mimetic. A desire for mimesis or a close-as-possible parroting turns out to be relatively boring, both to prepare and to read, whereas some sort of slip away from the original seems peculiarly fruitful. Each of the chapters in this book deals with a different sort of history and slippage from the mimetic into a poetic address closer to a salmon maneuver, or surprise.

Poetic address: I am thinking of Avital Ronell's reflection on the "Greeting" and how that fits—indeed, shapes—my idea of translation. For her, "the Greeting first establishes a distance so that proximity can occur. . . ." That distance subsists between the original and our rendering. Ronell quotes, in her contribution to "The Legacy of Jacques Derrida," his *Aporias*, that distance he marks in translation and the condition of the self: "Such a difference from and with itself would then be its very thing, the pragma of its pragmatics: the stranger at home, the invited or the one who is called" (Ronell 465). J. Hillis Miller, in the same collection, points out the essential call that Derrida would have the reader obey, in responding to the wholly other or "le tout autre" (Miller 483). We must all allow ourselves "to be greeted by the poem—that is to say, met or truly struck by it" (Ronell 18–19). Furthermore, "the Greeting is a staying behind but also a going along" (26). It is indeed like Derrida's idea, in his "Voyager avec," of traveling with, part of the discussions called *La Contre-allée: Dérive, arrivée, catastrophe*—"Voyager Avec": here the object of the preposition *avec*, "with," is left open, for all of us as readers, translators, travelers of texts, greeting and being greeted. Similarly, W. J. T. Mitchell invokes, in his *What Do Pictures Want?*, Louis Althusser's notion of "hailing" (49), and in the same volume reflects on the notions of othering, twinning, division, and yet uniting (as in the Twin Towers) and cloning (as in Dolly the sheep)—none of these reflections are foreign to the idea of translation (49, 22–25).

Now in this greeting, inner shape and personal voice are crucial. They must, both of them, leave room for an openness and question: the latter so crucial to Yves Bonnefoy's notion of translation, and both interdependent with the "room" that plays a major role in the book by William Gass, *Reading Rilke: Reflections on the Problems of Translation*. The poems of Rainer Maria Rilke have held out a fertile ground for some of the most talented translators, and this ground or room (*Raum*) Gass conceives as "the space made by Being's breathing" (37), an *Innerweltraum* (literally, an inner world space). In this breathing space of the poet's moving inside or "inwarding" (145), as Gass calls it, many different interpretations can find their own room. Discussing the translator's task, Gass states his belief in one kind of mimesis, that of the "delicate adjudications," equivalences, adjustments in the poem (89).

An initial reflection back at the parrot in the mirror: in a rendering of poetic repetition, whether rhymed or material. García Lorca's brief ode to the self deals with just that theme, indicated by the title: "Narciso." Here Narcissus staring at himself is first captured in a cloud of fragrance; he marvels at its emission by the other in himself and finally reflects that fragrance in his own rhyming sorrow and in the pond of reflection. The original Spanish fits this reflective form and function, perfectly self-enclosed:

> Narciso
> Tu olor
>
> · · · · · ·
>
> Narciso
> Mi dolor
> Y mi dolor mismo
> (54–56)

While the English, however fragrant, cannot ever capture such self-reflection as the "olor/dolor" rhyme, William Jay Smith's translation has captured both the heady whiff of the claustrophobic universe and the self-reflective fantasy, doomed to repetition and glorying in it:

> Narciso
> Your fragrance
> . . . . ,
> Narciso
> My sorrow
> And my sorrow's self
> (55–57)

The repeated *s* sounds—Narciso, sorrow, sorrow's self—compensate for the loss of the other rhyme, while the poem is balanced between other and same, yours and mine, myself and my self's self. The minimal reflection in the last line makes up for the rest, so that the self stares again at its emotion.

García Lorca's is a poem of address, as are many of the simplest and grandest poems of the French language. In them, the notions of layering can be crucial: one element of the poem may refer back to the past or on to the future, even as the person addressed is given that past and future, not just the present. For example, in Baudelaire's "Semper eadem," the original has included in its first line a reference to another time outside the present:

> "D'où vous vient, disiez-vous, cette tristesse étrange,
> Montant comme la mer sur le roc noir et nu?"
> (45)

This element both of past referral and personal recounting—"disiez-vous," "you used to say"—in no way extraneous to the poem, has been eliminated in a recent English translation:

> "You're like some rock the sea is swallowing—
> What is it that brings on these moods of yours?"
> (223)

A pity. For the shape of the translation to somewhat approximate, without servile imitation, that of the original, such complications of time and person might well be included.

The question of address is the kind that the inner shape of the poem as translated has to make room for. (I am saying *inner*, because the *outer* shape may vary: take Yves Bonnefoy's renderings of English poetry, that of Shakespeare, Keats, and Yeats—there are considerably more lines in the French than the English, even as the interior shape corresponds.) It is where the personal comes in. In my own case, it was my work on the poetry of the Provençal poet René Char that proved the most problematic. For in the split between the poet and his or her own text—that is, in my case, between Char as poet and as interpreter of his own texts—there were already two people for me to converse with. One of the basic problems was his desire for literalism, for the poem to be kept "face to the wave." Whatever that expression might have meant in its original, I translated it as a sort of word-for-wordness. So, for example, I felt summoned to use words I actually found too heavy, such as "bivouac" for the French *bivouaquer*, in his poem "L'Allégresse" ("Gladness").

> Les nuages sont dans les rivières, les torrents parcourent le ciel. Sans saisie les journées montent en graine, meurent en herbe. Le temps de la famine et celui de la moisson, l'un sous l'autre dans l'air haillonneux, ont effacé leur différence. Ils filent ensemble, ils bivaquent! (*Selected Poems* 106)

I continued to hear or to feel a lightness hovering around that text and wanted more than anything not to weigh it down. After a certain amount of argument with the poet, I managed "encamp"—but it was a struggle. Perhaps in each poem you love certain moments, and they are the ones you most want to get right: in this poem I loved the words "sans saisie," about the days unplucked, and so used "unpicked" for the harvest that was not gathered.

> Clouds are in the rivers, torrents course through the sky. Unpicked, the days run to seed, perish in the green. The time of famine and the time of harvest, one beneath the other in the tattered air, have wiped out their difference. They slip by together, they encamp! (*Selected Poems* 106–7)

Char's radically complex love poem "Le Visage nuptial," or "The Nuptial Countenance"—of a voluptuousness rare in French poetry of the early twentieth century—occasioned much discussion with the poet. It opens on a willed leave taking:

> A présent disparais, mon escorte, debout dans la distance;
> La douceur du nombre vient de se détruire.
>
> 〜
>
> Now let my escort disappear, standing in the distance;
> Numbers have just lost their sweetness.
> (*Selected Poems* 28–29)

The majestic slow beginning I had originally made even slower: "standing far off into the distance." But that was too distant.

> . . . .
> Tôt soustrait au flux des lésions inventives
> (La pioche de l'aigle lance haut le sang évasé)
> . . . .
> O voûte d'effusion sur la couronne de son ventre,
> Murmure de dot noire!
> . . . .
> Le soir a fermé sa plaie de corsaire où voyageaient les fusées vagues
>   parmi la peur soutenue des chiens.
> Au passé les micas du deuil sur ton visage.
> . . . .
> Prends, ma Pensée, la fleur de ma main pénétrable,
> Sens s'éveiller l'obscure plantation.
>
> 〜
>
> Soon subtracted from the flux of contriving lesions
> (the eagle's pickaxe flings high the flaring blood)
> O vaulted effusion upon the crown of her belly,
> murmurings of dark dowry!
> . . . .
> Evening has closed its corsair's gash where the rockets soared
>   aimlessly amid a dogged fear.
> Past now the micas of mourning on your face.
> . . . .
> Take, oh my Thought, the flower of my penetrable hand,

Feel the dark planting waken.
(*Selected Poems* 30–31)

Whew. I had delighted in finding the sharpness of "flings/flaring" for the eagle's pickaxe and worried a bit about the "dogged fear," whether I was losing the reality in the metaphor: "Fine," said Char, "I can still hear them barking." (I used to go to work with him on my motorbike; I had indeed been afraid of the dogs on the road near his house: that reality stuck.)

But the crucial question was to come: Did I know whose face it was? Know for whom he had written the poem, Char asked me. No, I said—and I cannot now remember whether or not I did. It was Greta Knutson, the wife of Tristan Tzara the Dadaist. Char stormed out into the kitchen, returned, placed his hand on my knee, and we continued our work. Now it happens that the beloved was blond, so what were the "murmure de dot noire" and later the "obscure plantation" doing there? "Poetic license," said the poet. Indeed. The feeling and sound of a strange nobility sensed in this erotic epic was hard to capture, as it led to the final statement: "This is . . . this [is]," in a certainty that called on the religious ritual of the bread and wine: "This is Christ's body. . . ."

> Voici le sable mort, voici le corps sauvé:
> La Femme respire; l'Homme se tient debout.
> ❧
> This is the sand dead, this the body saved:
> Woman breathes, Man stands upright.
> (*Selected Poems* 32–33)

The "debout" recalls the first line: "debout dans la distance," only now it is ultimate presence. How it used to bother me that the man stood upright after the sexual encounter, while she simply breathed. But no longer. For that's just what they did *in* this highly voluptuous love poem, whose address is interior, not turned toward the reader. Or the translator.

As for questions of address, they give rise to the thorny issue of gender. To whom and of whom is the poet speaking? A question not always easily resolved. One of the most challenging cases in my own experience turned around my own excessive psychological projection into one of Char's poems. To be sure, any woman translator involved in the translations of a great male poet could have made this error, in judgment and in poetry. It reflects a lack of imagination on my part, and a frankness on the part of the poet that might be instructive for others.

One of Char's love poems, "Allégeance," or "Allegiance," concerns the loss of a beloved one moving out into the world beyond, even as the lover keeps watch. The French begins:

> Dans les rues de la ville il y a mon amour. Peu importe où il va dans le temps divisé. Il n'est plus mon amour, chacun peut lui parler. Il ne se souvient plus; qui au juste l'aima? . . .

And ends, reaching far past the beginning question not by an answer but by a simple extension:

> Dans les rues de la ville il y a mon amour. Peu importe où il va dans le temps divisé. Il n'est plus mon amour, chacun peut lui parler, il ne se souvient plus; qui au juste l'aima et l'éclaire de loin pour qu'il ne tombe pas?

Looking too hastily at the words of the lover—"mon amour . . . il"—I first assumed that the object of "my love" was masculine, as the French seemed to be. I had forgotten entirely that since René Char was writing the poem, that was very far from the case. He was simply using the Elizabethan sense of "my love" as he pointed out subsequently, and so the absent one was, of course, a woman. I had already undertaken my translation before consulting the poet and had written:

> In the streets of the town goes my love. Small matter where he goes in divided time. He is no longer my love, anyone may speak with him. He remembers no longer, who exactly loved him?

Subsequently I had, in fact, published the translation using a compromise measure, both impersonalizing the love and ruining the translation:

In the streets of the town goes my love. Small matter where it moves in divided time. . . . (*Poems of René Char* 94–95)

Then, righting matters, I retranslated it in 1992 for a new publication, giving finally what the poet had intended:

In the streets of the town goes my love. Small matter where she moves in divided time. She is no longer my love, anyone may speak with her. She remembers no longer: who exactly loved her, and lights her from afar, lest she should fall? (*Selected Poems* 64–65)

Now in retranslating, twice, and republishing the poem, I finally came to feel that I had lost some of my closeness to it. It was not speaking with my voice. The translator is not, naturally, to be included in the picture, and yet I had so identified with the whole situation that I was there. I believe in personal criticism, but that is one thing, and the personal translation I had unknowingly indulged in was another matter entirely. The lesson I learned was quite simply one of imagination, not one of imitation. I had merged voices and vectored them in the wrong direction.

An associated, if different, problem with translating this powerful poet arose with my translation of his poem "The Swift." Here the bird had to be called not "it," as one would say in ordinary language and as I had first written, but "he," for the personal strength of the poem to come across. I needed the warmth of feeling that the personal pronoun implied, not just because it was a question of love, but even in the animal world. Char was a poet who added milk to the figs outside his window so that the birds could nourish themselves properly in a dry winter. Yet again, I changed my translation, in consultation with the poet. But this time it was my choice, not his.

Martinet aux ailes trop larges, qui vire et crie sa joie autour de la maison. Tel est le coeur.

. . . .

Il n'est pas d'yeux pour le tenir. Il crie, c'est toute sa présence. Un mince fusil va l'abattre. Tel est le coeur.

&

Swift with wings too wide, wheeling and shrieking his joy as he circles the house. Such is the heart.

. . . .

No eyes can hold him. He shrieks for his only presence. A slight
gun is about to fell him. Such is the heart.

(*Selected Poems* 58–59)

Since in French there had already been the conjoining of personal
and animal in the "il," it was in English that changing the pronoun
changed the poem. Here the three people were the poet, the first
translator, and that translator taking a later look, reinterpreting.

Allied to this question and to that of address and participation
is that of the French pronoun *on*. The minute an English speaker or
translator might be tempted to say "one" is a fatal minute, in my view.
In fact, however, this is one of those turning points that, taxing the
patience, tests the flexibility. Take the brief poem of Pierre Reverdy,
"Quand on n'est pas de ce monde." It seemed just right to render the
title as literally identical: "When One Is Not of This World," whereas
in the other uses of the pronoun, it seemed more sensible to vary the
effect.

Il y eut, tout le temps que dura l'orage, quelqu'un qui parla sous le
couvert. Autour de la lumière que traçait son doigt sur la nappe on
aurait pu voir de grosses lettres noires. . . . La voix semblait venir de
derrière. On ne savait pas si c'était le mur ou le paravent. Les lettres
disparurent ou plutôt elles s'étaient réunies et formaient un nom
étrange qu'on ne déchiffrait pas. (114)

ૐ

There was, all the time the storm lasted, someone speaking under
cover. Around the light his finger traced on the tablecloth, large black
letters would have been visible to anyone looking hard. . . . The voice
seemed to come from behind, whether the wall or the screen, no one
knew. The letters disappeared or rather they had merged, forming a
strange and undecipherable name. (115)

Retaining the "one" in other terms—no one, anyone, someone—
would retain the collective sense of the pronoun and still take off
some of the freeze. Thus, for "on aurait pu voir," I gave "visible to
anyone looking," wanting to preserve the generality of the French
but at less remove. For "on ne savait pas," I chose "no one knew"
for exactly the same reason and to balance the effect. And finally,

I omitted the *on* in the case of the odd "un nom étrange qu'on ne déchiffrait," which became, for me, "forming a strange and undecipherable name." The word "undecipherable" seemed able to capture the strangeness: it needed to be strikingly long and sufficiently peculiar in order to fit that phrasing.

It is often a question of what kind of distance one wants to create or preserve, or then transgress. In Reverdy's poem "Mouvant paysage" ("Moving Landscape"), the verbs are almost all controlled by an *on*, the distancing of which I wished not to imitate: I preferred to have the warmth of a personal inclusion, giving the reader a place, like the translator, in the poem. This decision is, however, one of those that changes the tone of the text, so it has to be made with full knowledge of what one is—that is, what I am or we are—doing:

> Levé
> Le chant plus haut
>
> On part
> . . . . . .
> Peut-on savoir l'heure qu'il est
> Aucune limite n'est fixée
> On pourrait traverser la terre
> sans jamais s'arrêter
> . . . .
> Et l'on n'entend plus rien
> Un passant
> Une étoile tombe
> Et les autres qui la regardent
> La lune tord son cou par-dessus les arbres

My rendering reads:

> Risen
> The song higher
>
> We are leaving
> . . . .
> What time is it please
> No limit has been fixed

We could cross the earth
without ever stopping.
. . . .
We hear nothing now
  A passerby
  A star is falling
And the others looking at it
The moon cranes its neck above the trees
(152)

The rising song announces the rest of the text with a joy that a
"lifted" voice seemed to me unable to convey. Here we are in the
scene, whether we will or not. Reading more of Reverdy gives us the
freedom to interpret this text along with others, plunging the reader
into the center of things not necessarily understood.

One of the more complicated issues of this sort arose in my translation of *Ostinato*, the poetic prose masterpiece by Louis-René des
Forêts. The person speaking in this text is not an "I" but a "one" or
a "he." The choice of the third-person pronoun in a language like
French for a life lived in the first person is a choice at once strange
and impressive. Eliminating the person concerned is disconcerting
for the readers' habits of projection. To put such a pressure on ordinary recounting strikes the reader as particularly odd in the case
of an author so obsessed in his other texts by a voice speaking to
excess, as in *Le Bavard*, and by silence in the text and the world, by
a muting and a soundlessness. Here is what he says of this decision,
which I simply quoted in my preface so as to explain the feeling I
had to convey in the translation, through which neither des Forêts
nor, of course, myself was sensed as speaking:

> The third person to affirm itself against the default of the first one. He
> is what I was, not what I am which has no real presence. Unless one
> wants to see in it the unique and ultimate recourse to eliminate one's
> own person.
>
> No, it isn't himself nor myself, rather it's the world speaking.
> That's its terrible beauty. (des Forêts 66)

The omission of a pronoun can be a powerful ploy toward the feeling
of inclusion. Take the concluding line of Hugo von Hofmannsthal's

poem "Unendliche Zeit" ("Infinite Time"), in which the original reads literally "It appeared to me" ("War mir"):

> In mich hätt ich gesogen dein zwanzigjähriges Dasin
> —War mir, indessen der Baum noch seine Tropfen behielt.

The superb translation by Michael Hamburger simply renders the appearance as a far-reaching phenomenon, eliminating the first-person viewer from the second line. Although it is understood, from the context, that the narrator is the viewer ("mich . . . mir"), the generality manages to extend the feeling outward:

> I had absorbed within me your twenty-year-old existence
> While—so it seemed—still the tree held all its raindrops unshed.
> (333–34)

Slippage must not interfere with the essential—which is to say, *conceptual*—shape of the poem, inward as that might be. Just as in Proust's great novel, it is crucial to begin and end with the word "time," so a poem conceived as a rondo, in the round, should commence and finish in the same place.

The baroque poets were especially keen on this kind of completion, and Jean de Sponde's celebrated *Sonnets de la mort*, his stanzas about death, show how the self-enclosure of the poem serves to distinguish it from the rest of life. It is death's lesson, as we could call it, that brings full circle the life cycle, at the far end of which, as the two meet up, we must die:

> Mais si faut-il mourir, et la vie orgueilleuse
> Qui brave de la mort, sentira ses fureurs . . .

It begins, at the birth of the poem:

> Yet we must die, and proud life,
> That so mocks death, will yet feel its furies . . .

The "mais" seems to enter into argument, to stand against some unspoken but suggested proposition about our living, perhaps hoping against hope that there will be exceptions. "J'ai vu," continues the poet, I have seen all this, lightning and thunder and the snow melting, I have seen torrents dry up, have seen snarling lions grown tame . . . so:

Vivez, hommes, vivez, mais si faut-il mourir.

Concluding in identical manner, it makes its own point all the more strongly for the opposition being only implicit. The essential part of the English, then, is to make that rendering sufficiently strong to withstand the repetition:

Live, men, live, yet man must die. (160–61)

Thus the deadly warning repeats, first in an incipit and then in an exit, with its other part always in shadow. The poetic paradox that the desire to live is what is implicit or shadowed, while the necessity of dying is what is highlighted and explicit, is part of the baroque contrast.

As for the translation of the ending, another quite splendid example of more or less the same period could be taken from the great Spanish baroque poet Luis de Góngora. This is one of the classic poems that sets up a comparison between the beloved and nature, the latter, in spite of her well-known beauties, falling (of course) short. The sun cannot compare, though it might like to, with the beloved's golden tresses:

Mientras por competir con tu cabello
oro bruñido el Sol relumbra en vano,
mientras con menosprecio en medio el llano
mira tu blanca frente el lilio bello;

mientras a cada labio, por cogello,
siguen más ojos que al clavel temprano,
y mientras triunfa con desdén Lozano
del luciente cristal tu gentil cuello;

goza cuello, cabello, labio y frente,
antes que lo que fue en tu edad dorada
oro, lilio, clavel, cristal luciente,

no solo en plata o vïola troncada
se vuelva, mas tú y ello juntamente
en tierra, en humo, en polvo, en sombra, en nada.

&⁊

While to compete with your hair,
The sun, like burnished gold shines all in vain
while your white forehead disdains the lily lovely in the plain

while each lip is watched by more eyes
to pluck it, than the early carnation
and while your delicate neck surpasses
the shining crystal with fair disdain,

neck hair, lip, and forehead
take your pleasure before what used to be
gold, lily, carnation, shining crystal
not only turns to silver or cut violet

but you and they together turn
to earth, smoke, dust, shadow, nothing.
(212–13)

The palest lilies are compared with the white of her forehead, the rose with her red lips, and so on, in the standard form *abcd*. But at the end, when the poetically expected undoing—the mortal turn—takes place among all the living elements, the rush toward disintegration takes place exactly in a reversal of elements, *dcba*, in steady dematerialization, leading to the final term:

en tierra, en humo, en polvo, en sombra, en nada.

&⁊

to earth, smoke, dust, shadow, nothing.

In translation, the final word must be strong enough, as "nada" indeed is, to have the whole panoply of beauty dissolve into it. For this, the English "nothing" is sufficient, whereas "nothingness," as some translator might have put it, is not.

to earth, smoke, dust, shadow, nothingness.

Here the suffix "-ness" would have weakened the terror of the ending, undoing the singular strength of nothing, reducing it to the level of generality, since so many things adjectival can find a verbal form in "-ness"—for example, kindness or blindness. Particularly awkward would be the increase from the monosyllabic first three elements—earth, smoke, dust—and the next bisyllabic "shadow," which I prefer to "shade," to the heavy trisyllabic ending, so I would far prefer to end here with "nothing."

In much the same era and the same vein, in the German baroque poem by Andreas Gryphius "An sich Selbst," the final undoing reaches high melodrama:

> Und eine Not muss uns mit allem Vorsatz töten.

Ending with this verbal death gives fate its due, and the poem, its aesthetic drama. Alas, in one English version, a slight shift in order undoes not the human so much as the poem:

> One curse with all design must slay us through its terrors. (252)

Of course, the word "terrors" is properly terrifying but scarcely poetic in last place, where I would have preferred to find the verb, as in the original: "through its terrors slay us."

An effective rhyme always seems to me to retain something of a miracle. Take Guillaume Apollinaire's "Adieu." The five lines are grouped by rhyme *abaab*, in a farewell at once melancholy, floral, and unfixed:

> J'ai cueilli ce brin de bruyère
> L'automne est morte souviens-t'en
> Nous ne nous verrons plus sur terre
> Odeur du temps brin de bruyère
> Et souviens-toi que je t'attends

Roger Shattuck's English translation manages to retain the "heather" with the cohering element "together," so that, in fact, the whole poem does stay together, through that fragile purple sprig:

> I picked this fragile sprig of heather

Autumn has died long since remember
Never again shall we see one another
Odor of time sprig of heather
Remember I await our life together
(86–87)

This is a case in which another text feels present: Victor Hugo's brief lament for his drowned daughter, "Demain, dès l'aube" ("Tomorrow, at Dawn"), dated September 3, 1847, in which the poet sets out toward her grave ("Vois-tu, je sais que tu m'attends"; "see, I know you are waiting for me") (Hugo 51), placing upon it some flowering heather, "bruyère en fleur," whose fragrance perfumes this poem also. Again, this is a poem of address: we might have imagined the poet speaking to his mistress, alive—until he reaches the tomb, when we might have imagined her dead. Upon its being instead his young daughter hangs the profound emotion of the poem. As so often happens, this surprise is at the very end: that is how it works.

IV. *Mallarmé in England and at Home*

WHISTLER

STÉPHANE MALLARMÉ HIMSELF was a translator. Sometimes, as in his translation of the famous "Ten O'Clock" lecture by his American friend James Abbott McNeill Whistler, he was greatly aided by others. If Mallarmé himself wanted so much to translate the piece, it was not only because he shared Whistlerian convictions, but because Whistler represented in English quite exactly the poetic spirit of Mallarmé himself. In a shared language of artistic suggestion and aesthetic conviction, they had, from the beginning and faultlessly to the end, a meeting of souls. If Mallarmé complained of his *Hérodiade* that it left him sterile, being such a solitary work, the collaborative venture that the translation of the "Ten O'Clock" lecture turned out to be was the perfect foil for that solitariness (letter to Lefébure, July 1865; *Selected Letters* 54). Involving four people, it was a collaboration between the American, or rather the English, language and the French and, second, between artists and poets of America, England, Ireland, and France.

Mallarmé called upon the services of a Virginian called Francis Viélé-Griffin to help him out with the translation. Yet there is a slippage on two counts here. First, in the appearance of the text: Mallarmé's request for the same spacing as in the original was not followed. The typography is different from the English version, without its airiness in printing that Whistler had cared so much about: "son aération," said Mallarmé, who himself cared greatly about presentation, as we see in his influential "Un Coup de dés jamais n'abolira le hasard" ("A Throw of Dice Never Will Abolish Chance") printed, in various scripts and sizes, in the journal *Cosmopolis* in 1897. The second problem is that of the signature itself. Viélé-Griffin's name was to have been added to Mallarmé's as initials only, so his name would not be, said Mallarmé, repeated to the point of irritation. On the same day (April 25, 1888), Mallarmé wrote to Whistler on the topic to determine if he had any objection to adding the name of Viélé-Griffin. Be frank in your answer, he wrote. "First of all, things have to suit you in this matter" (*Correspondance*, 14).

Initially, he had hesitated over adding Viélé-Griffin's name. What Whistler thought, we do not know; it is after this that Whistler came to Paris to confer on the translation, accompanied by the Irishman George Moore, and it is possible that he objected to the other signature at this point. It is all mysterious, this signing and de-signing of someone else's name. Perhaps Whistler *did* prefer to have only his name associated with that of the great French poet, and it is perhaps on his initiative and not that of Mallarmé that Viélé-Griffin's name was removed. In any case, this translation by four persons is marked with only Mallarmé's name. Be that as it may, the "Ten O'Clock" lecture left, said Mallarmé, "a lively impression on all sides." He was delighted to have done "this little work" of translation, so pleasing to Whistler:

> I did it as I would have for myself, naturally, and it was all the easier since I was in complete sympathy with your vision of Art. Thank you for understanding the least of my efforts, but especially for the absolutely precious aid with the details that you are giving me afterwards, detailed and with such lovely precision that I have already profited from it. (May 7 or 13, 1888; *Correspondance* 18)

As for the difficulties of this particular text, they do not seem excessive, compared with the difficulties of translating Mallarmé into English. In the other direction, Mallarmé himself certainly botched the job when he tried translating a sonnet by his beloved Edgar Allan Poe, making the translators among us feel much better.

The very famous—indeed, infamous—"Ten O'Clock" lecture was first given at the Prince's Hall in London at the unusual hour of 10 p.m. on February 20, 1885, because Whistler wanted to be sure everyone had eaten dinner and would be in a receptive mood. His title had to remain, even in French, "Ten O'Clock," because translating the time as "vingt-deux heures" would give it the sound of a train schedule. The lecture occasioned some excitement and still more confusion on both sides of the Channel. Mallarmé was intrigued by, among many other things in "Ten O'Clock," Whistler's ironic and stabbing words so neatly aimed with equal force against professors, collectors, and art historians:

> There are those also, sombre of mien, and wise with the wisdom of books, who frequent museums and burrow in crypts; collecting—comparing—compiling—classifying—contradicting. . . .
> Careful in scrutiny are they, and conscientious of judgment—establishing, with due weight, unimportant reputations—discovering the picture, by the stain on the back—testing the torso, by the leg that is missing—filling folios with doubts on the way of that limb—disputatious and dictatorial, concerning the birthplace of inferior persons—speculating, in much writing, upon the great worth of bad work. (148–49)

As well as these "true clerks of the collection," who "mix memoranda with ambition" and "reduce Art to statistics," there is the professor or appointed preacher, who doesn't come off any better than the art historian:

> He stands in high places—harangues and holds forth.
> Sage of the Universities—learned in many matters, and of much experience in all, save his subject.
> Exhorting—denouncing—directing.
> Filled with wrath and earnestness.
> Bringing powers of persuasion, and polish of language, to prove—nothing.
> Torn with much teaching—having naught to impart.
> Impressive—important—shallow.
> Defiant—distressed—desperate.
> (149–50)

This lecture—funny, angry, and deeply serious—includes the credo of craft. The artist chooses to be "set apart" not just from the teacher so somber and so bookish, but from everyone in general. Standing "in no relation to the moment," the painter becomes "a monument of isolation—hinting at sadness" and creates, specifically, a *"painter's poetry."* Of course, Mallarmé, with his refusal of the herd mentality, would agree with such a position.

Here Whistler waxes at once biblical in style and poetic in his incantations, as he sings the artist going forth, in the anaphoric mode of a litany: "And when . . . And presently . . . And with the power of creation . . . And the toilers tilled . . . and the heroes returned . . . And time . . . And the people . . ." (140–41). Yet the people should have nothing to say about creation, says the deeply undemocratic Whistler. The worst is when they do, as now, and art mingles with crass commerce, represented by its cities: "And the people—this time—had much to say in the matter—and all were satisfied. And Birmingham and Manchester arose in their might—and Art was relegated to the curiosity shop" (142).

The "Ten O'Clock" lecture is not a people's pronouncement, but rather a manifesto of self-exaltation: "The holiday-maker rejoices in the glorious day, and the painter turns aside to shut his eyes. . . . False again, the fabled link between the grandeur of Art and the glories and virtues of the State, for Art feeds not upon nations, and peoples may be wiped from the face of the earth, but Art *is*" (155). Like everything about Whistler and his work, "Ten O'Clock" is irritating, hilarious, and convincing. In its radical mix of styles, it forms a superb example of an extended prose poem, certainly one of the most peculiar pieces ever written by a visual artist.

Mallarmé was delighted by the publication, especially its presentation: at the end of each marginal gloss, Whistler had placed his butterfly signature, with the butterfly posed in various ways to mark his different moods. Mallarmé loved it all:

> What a treasure! it's worth one of your frames; and, on the inside, it's completely Whistler, ah, ah! when I show it to everyone, they marvel, like me. . . . The letters, even without the volution of the irascible and exquisite butterfly (sometimes it frightens me with its tail) are traced exactly with the same point as your etchings. (*Correspondance* 62)

He was equally amused by Whistler's account of the Ruskin trial, reading it over and over aloud: "Quelle représentation idéale!" In particular, he thanked Whistler for using his name in the margin of a text attacking Oscar Wilde: "And thanks for my name, which I discovered in front of everything; to be placed like that by you, my dear Whistler, was very comforting" (*Correspondance* 62). He found the appearance of his own name *included* in a work of Whistler's as appealing as his own use of Whistler's name in the rhyme of the "Billet à Whistler," commissioned by the painter for an issue of the *Whirlwind*, was to Whistler. Their names and works went well together, and that juncture sealed their friendship.

In Mallarmé's translation of Whistler, the editor had of his own initiative changed Mallarmé's "cheval vapeur" to a "cheval-machine" for Whistler's "steam horse," but there were a few more mistakes than that. Whistler, who said the French form was ideal, was all the same bothered over the loss in translation of a few of his deliberate ambiguities: "one or two passages where the subtlety of ideas to be expressed and perhaps the way they were expressed caused a certain ambiguity of possible meaning" (*Correspondance* 16). The poet of ambiguities had, thought Whistler, flattened out some expressions into French clarity. This they discussed in Paris, to the evident satisfaction of both, with George Moore sharing in the consultation (20). A few changes were made at this point. For example, Whistler's "Art is upon the Town!"—which had initially been rendered as "L'Art sévit sur la ville," becomes "L'Art court les rues" (135). As Mallarmé pointed out, he could not very well have put "L'Art fait le trottoir," as if she were a prostitute. (It is the English of this expression that is erroneously listed in the 1945 Pléiade edition on page 1603 as "Art is not the tours." For the changes made in the French translation after Mallarmé's first rendering, when it was reviewed by Whistler and Moore, see the appendix to the Barbier edition of the Whistler-Mallarmé correspondence.) Some interesting details of the translation include the rendering of the expression "dreading exposure" as, first, a dread of the metaphoric "éclat" and, finally, a term that opts for the concrete reality: "nudité." And in a passage about the artist as a man apart, tracing "strange devices with a burnt stick upon a gourd," Whistler maintains that "gourde," not "coupe," must be used, opting again for the literal.

Whistler's sense of and sensitivity to language are surprisingly acute, no less so than that of Mallarmé himself. In any case, Whistler leaves with a copy of the *Faun*, bearing the signature of

Son ami (et collaborateur)
Stéphane Mallarmé, 1888,

as if indeed this cross-the-Channel translation were to have sealed their friendship, like drinking from the same gourd.

Mallarmé liked to have his name linked with Whistler's, even, as he said, should it appear beneath that of the American. He wrote elsewhere to Whistler how happy he was to have a chance to put "mon nom au-dessous du vôtre" ("my name beneath yours"), and subsequently, on May 23, he insisted to the printer that when his name appeared on a poster advertising the translation, "let it be in very small type, so that I not seem to be profiting from the Exhibition for my own good. . . . All the attention should be drawn to Whistler's name" (*Correspondance* 6). Repeatedly, they are both delighted to have their names *figure* in each other's texts: Whistler in Mallarmé's *Médaillon* or portrait of him; Mallarmé in Whistler's margins, underneath his translations, or on his poster in small type.

Mallarmé was, as witnesses tell us, intrigued by Whistler's oddness, independence, and wit from the first moment. He had probably met him initially with Théodore Duret in 1886–87, subsequently in Manet's studio, and then again through Monet (*Correspondance* 6). Whistler had, with great temerity, invited Monet to exhibit in December 1887 with the Royal Society of British Artists, over which he presided in a totally dictatorial fashion. (This invitation was to rankle with the members and was in part responsible for Whistler's being voted out as president; 57–81, esp. 72.) When Whistler was to meet Monet in Paris one Sunday morning, Monet invited Mallarmé to join them for lunch at the Café de la Paix. That is one of the elements in the certain start of the friendship between poet and painter, soldered shortly thereafter by their joint effort in the French rendering of Whistler's English "Ten O'Clock," a friendship that was to last until death.

Mallarmé's grasp of Whistler's real statements, made in his conception for the few who understood, was greatly helped by their shared interest in the Orient. It was not, as it never is in the best translations, simply a matter of rendering Whistler's actual "language," but also his attitude and aesthetic, his moral outlook. What Mallarmé could render so well as a French form of orientalism, because it matched his characteristic way of thinking and his vocabulary, was a kind of *Japonisme* whose way through his own personal prism was lit by his attitude toward suggestiveness, ellipsis, and focus. It worked because the recognition was right.

A few salient characteristics are shared by Japanese art and the art of these two masters of suggestion. First and most essential, that of lightness: Mallarmé's celebrated verses on envelopes and on fans weigh not more than the signature of the butterfly. Then, the frequent cropping off of the principal figure, textual or visual, in media res, so that the reader or viewer feels plunged into the immediacy of the scene or action. Next, there is a subtle repetition in the pattern, as opposed to any more obvious contrast. Writing to the painter Henri Fantin-Latour in 1868, Whistler described his use of the repetitive technique, a description equally pertinent to a Mallarmé sonnet:

> It seems to me that colour ought to be, as it were, embroidered on the canvas, that is to say, the same colour ought to appear in the picture continually here and there, in the same way that a thread appears in an embroidery, and so should all the others, more or less according to their importance. Look how well the Japanese understood this. They never look for contrast, on the contrary, they're after repetition. (Holden 13)

Crucial among the shared techniques is the oriental mode of off-centering, as opposed to an occidental way of placing the central focus *at the center*. But the main element in their poetic likeness is their stress on deliberate understatement, suggestiveness, and negative space. In this, Mallarmé's famous rose "absente de tous les bouquets" ("missing from all the bouquets") is like Whistler's bare seascapes; in both cases, we see the nineteenth-century summit of minimalist art.

As Donald Holden so well describes Whistler's use of space, particularly at the water's edge:

> Here space becomes a subject in itself, continuous, ambiguous, dissolving objects in a diffused light that abolishes edges, defies

interruption and insists on becoming a field of modulated color, a field of paint. (19)

Holden also points out how Whistler's choice of nighttime permitted the blurring of edges, the shading of figure into background. On the lighter side, this leaving of space permits aeration; more gravely, the inclusion of emptiness has philosophic overtones, present in both the artist and the poet as symbolists.

TENNYSON

The partnership of Mallarmé and Whistler was a fine one in translation and in the tradition of friendship. But 'twas not always the way with Mallarmé. For a strange thing occurs—very peculiar, indeed—in Mallarmé's own translation, unaided, of a great English poet, Alfred Lord Tennyson. I think of this incident, singular and lasting over almost twenty years, as Mallarmé retranslating, and find in it a great surprise.

In the October 1874 issue of Mallarmé's *La Dernière Mode* (*The Latest Fashion*; *Prose* 79–94)—that two-year run of a journal entirely written by the Master himself, under many disguises, running the scale from "Madame de Ponty," "Mademoiselle Satin," and "Olympia la négresse," to "IX, le chef de chez Brabant, et al.," and a cast of invented readers, eager to know what to wear and prepare and how best to travel—there appeared his translation of Tennyson's "Mariana" of 1830. Only the last stanza had appeared previously, in *La Revue Indépendante*, in February of that year. Mallarmé had just finished translating several Poe poems, and the editors of this first Pléiade edition of Mallarmé's works comment that Mallarmé reveals himself as a rather indifferent and weak translator, "un traducteur assez incertain" (*Oeuvres* [1945] 1622). They continue their speculation by supposing that he had to fill a space in this number of *La Dernière Mode* hastily, so he just grabbed his translation of this Tennyson poem and thrust it in, wherever it would fit. It is unlikely, to be sure, that the readers, real or invented, would have known what to make of this very un-French text.

Mallarmé was a famous gatherer of friends, that is, of his circle, on his celebrated "Mardis" or Tuesday evenings, when he would lean on the mantel and hold forth—but he was also a gatherer of names. As Jeffrey Mehlman points out in his "Mallarmé and 'Seduction Theory,' " Mallarmé had already, if awkwardly, telescoped the names of Salomé and Hérodiade in his *Noces d'Hérodiade*, of which only one scene was published in his lifetime. This was, he thought, to be his masterpiece, which he requested his wife and daughter to destroy upon his death ("Believe me," he said with his last breath, "it would have been very beautiful"). Mehlman maintains that this Salomé/Hérodiade, a repressive (if dance-prone) heroine, has a twin sister in Lady Godiva, celebrated in another of Tennyson's poems, also translated by Mallarmé, not once but twice, like "Mariana" itself. He was clearly into retranslation.

The story goes like this: Georges Rochegrosse, who was perhaps planning to do a portrait of the Lady of Chester, asked Mallarmé, who had made a spontaneous oral translation of Tennyson's "Godiva," to write it out for him, which Mallarmé did, sending it almost by return mail (Steinmetz 356), proving that he knew his Tennyson. In response to Mallarmé's "Godiva," Philoxène Boyer, a friend of the painter Rochegrosse, exclaimed: "That is Tennyson himself in his thought and his very essence" ("dans sa pensée et dans sa moelle") (*Oeuvres* [1945] 1622). Mallarmé was scarcely "an uncertain translator" to all eyes. The reader may well recognize in the Tennyson poem just those accents that would most likely have appealed to Mallarmé, such as the following:

> The deep air listened round her as she rode,
> And all the low wind hardly breathed for fear.
> (Tennyson, II, 175)

Of course, Mallarmé recognized in this sonorous language what he was longing for in his own tongue. These were indeed those tones that the English had forgotten to recognize, as they were always innate to it. As he says of Tennyson in his memorial portrait, "Tennyson, vu d'ici" ("Tennyson, Seen from Here"), for an Edinburgh newspaper, some two weeks after his death in 1892:

> To have given to the human voice such intonations as had never before been heard (without Tennyson, a certain music befitting to the English nation would be lacking, as I see it) and to have made the national

instrument yield such new harmonies, instantly recognized as innate to it, constitutes the poet by his task and prestige. (*Prose* 73)

Now Mehlman's interest here is in the contrast between the "massive return of the repressed" in Salomé/Hérodiade as opposed to the "progressive and activist ego [of] Godiva" (108), and in their double reflection on death. The interwoven deaths of Mallarmé's mother and his sister Maria give rise to a long meditation on the interrelation of the heroines and on the relation of death to seduction. But my own reflection on Godiva on her horse leads me in a less dark direction. The first thing we *see* in anyone's speaking of Godiva is this capillary curtain, her loosened locks, as she showers down her "rippled ringlets to her knee," so as to be clothed in her curls and her chastity. (Elizabeth Gitter treats the serpentine hair of the seductress Vivien in "Merlin and Vivien" and the bartered golden ringlets of the woman in "The Ringlet" as they are "bought and sold, sold, sold," as part of a pervasive hair fetishism and taboo within the male Victorian imaginary [946].)

Mallarmé's own fascination with tresses is well documented (see his poem on "La Chevelure," beginning: "La Chevelure vol d'une flamme à l'extrême / Occident de désirs pour la tout déployer" [*Oeuvres* (1945) 53]; "Hair the flight of an extreme flaming / West with desire to spread it all out"), with its own titular recall of Baudelaire's two poems, in prose and verse, on "La Chevelure" ("The Mane of Hair"). Mallarmé, fascinated by the notion of and the sight of hair in general and in particular, remains terrified of Hérodiade's Medusa-like "massive" head of hair, just as he is of the forest. Everything enters into this madness of the mane, from Baudelaire's *élucubrations* on Jeanne Duval's abundant hair, curly as that of sheep ("O toison, moutonnant") in the verse version of "La Chevelure" (Baudelaire 26–27) and prose ("Un Hémisphère dans une chevelure"; "A Hemisphere in a Mane of Hair" [300–301]), through Mallarmé's own "La Chevelure" (*Oeuvres* [1945] 53) and the "naked hair" ("la chevelure nue") of an untitled sonnet beginning with an evocation of an ancient East (224). Then his "Plainte d'automne" ("Autumn Lament")— where he dreams of his dead Maria, reads Latin poems, and thrusts his hand deep into the fur of his cat, that "pure animal" (270)— suggests the pure but rather creepy "curls of Baby Jesus" on a doll made out of sugar or wax on the Christmas tree planned for an Alsatian reader in *La Dernière Mode* (*Prose* 94).

All this sends us back to Eugène Lefébure's famous letter to Mallarmé in 1862, ironically signaling the difference between his addressee's poetry and poetic outlook and those of the English laureate, as well as the difference in their coiffure, Tennyson's locks being curlier than Mallarmé's (*Oeuvres* [1945] 1622; see n. 2). One photograph of Mallarmé in 1863 (Steinmetz, between 176–77) shows how straight his hair could appear: his ringlets are saved for writing.

That letter inaugurates explicitly what was an implicit relation of Mallarmé to Tennyson, whom he admired: a one-sided admiration, which stretched over thirty years, from Lefébure's letter and Mallarmé's publication of his translation of Tennyson's "Mariana," in *La Dernière Mode* on October 18, 1874; through Mallarmé's translation, first oral, then written, of Tennyson's "Godiva," in 1884; Mallarmé's retranslation of "Mariana" in 1890 (thus, sixteen years later: speaking of retranslation!); then the interview with Mallarmé about Tennyson, printed on October 8, 1892; and the final memorial text in 1892.

A recent commentator about this thirty-year stretch has pointed out Lefébure's ironic statement in 1865 concerning the two poets, their writing, and their hair: "It is hard to imagine that Mallarmé and Tennyson spent fifty years (1842–92) on the same planet. . . ." But, he continues, no matter how trivial Mallarmé's subject matter (face cream, biking costumes), "it's not difficult to remember why deeply unfrivolous poets such as Valéry and Celan saw Mallarmé as a master, if not the master" (Mallarmé, *Selected Letters* 24).

Lady Godiva's nakedness is the ultimate surprise. On her unforgettable ride, the loosened locks she has wrapped about her to cover her nudity form a curtain, which the human eye penetrates at its peril, thus the peeping Tom finds his eyes shriveled. Mallarmé's meditation on vision, in the poet Yves Bonnefoy's words, allies itself with his affection for the night and disaffection for the day ("La Poétique" 15): even as daytime vision is associated with the despoiling of the essential mystery of poetic obscurity. As Mallarmé put it in a letter to François Coppée (April 20, 1868), "As for me, it's been two years now since I committed the sin of seeing the Dream in its ideal nakedness, whereas I should have been amassing between it

FIGURE 1. Stéphane Mallarmé, cover of *La Dernière Mode* (October 18, 1874).

and me a mystery of music and oblivion" (*Selected Letters* 84). There is spying and there is seeing, and poetic seeing through: the music and its mystery form a protective curtain against unworthy—read unpoetic—invasion. This may include the photographic: Bonnefoy has meditated, at length, on what photography does to painting, to poetry, and to us all, by the undoing of mysteriousness and the invasion by someone else. Since it reveals in such detail, it manifests its own distance, as if we were invaded by "an *other* . . . a no-one-knows-what other, on whom nothing you try to say takes any hold. . . . Non-meaning has penetrated human meaning. . . . Someone in us wonders . . . who?" ("Igitur and the Photographer," part 1, 21).

So Godiva enters into Mallarmé's poetic scheme of thought. But then why Mariana? First of all, given Mallarmé's fascination with groupings of all sorts, we cannot fail to appreciate such an extraordinary concatenation of *names*: his dead sister Maria and his wife Maria—both called Marie—then his mistress Méry Laurent (whose name was mispronounced "Mary" by her protector, the American dentist Dr. Evans), Marianne of the French Republic, and so on (Steinmetz 602). The name cannot have been without its importance, rendering the figure of Mariana and *La Dernière Mode* in which she so figures an even tighter fit. The golden-haired Méry was of bounteous proportions, and as Mallarmé pointed out in a letter to Lefébure, he only liked "one sort of fat woman; certain blond courtesans, in sunlight, especially wearing a black dress—women who seem to shine with all the life they have taken from men . . ." (*Selected Letters* 80). (See the photograph of Méry Laurent, in Steinmetz, facing page 177.) Around the name of Mariana was thus gathered a bevy of other women close to the Master, whose roles he could assume one after the other, while retaining his masterly mystery. That was precisely what he was doing in *La Dernière Mode*.

Now Mallarmé's initial rendering in poetic prose of Tennyson's "Mariana" was printed as "Figures d'album no. 1," but there was, contrary to expectation, to be no "Figures d'album no. 2." This translation and indeed this figure turned out to be a one-time venture, and the translation was retouched and recast by him in June 1890 for *Le Mercure de France*. It is the latter version that is reprinted in the Mondor and Jean-Aubry edition (*Oeuvres* [1945] 730), with the comment by Rémy de Gourmont that Mallarmé had touched it up for the new edition: "Le maître, en nous la laissant reproduire, a voulu, toujours si soigneux artiste, revoir et retoucher son travail d'alors" ("The master, permitting us to reproduce it, wanted, as the always careful artist he was, to look at it again and touch up his work") (1622). The reworking of the original rendering, whatever its merit as a translation, has something extremely odd about it. Perhaps it is, as Mondor and Jean-Aubry would have it (1621), a rather weak text; but, all the same, it is a prose poem, bearing several of the same organizing features as Tennyson's famous poem, while having to find, like all prose poems, its cohering principle from within to compensate for its lack of verse, rhyme, and unremarkable visual shape.

Michael Riffaterre has posited three necessary conditions for the prose poem, all of which together compensate for the loss of the formal features of verse: the invariance or equivalence of elements; their coextension with the text, defining it "as a formal unit" (117); and the presence of the significance beneath the surface meaning. What is triggered by whatever anomaly the reader may sense as a block to understanding in the text is a recognition of some intertext, something read or seen before or after the study of the text and found in the reader's mind. A syllepsis, or a word interpretable in two senses, often gives the clue to this intertext and to the interdependence of the two texts: present and remembered.

How might this work in the case of a translation, when the original and the translation are necessarily in an interdependent relation and, more complicated still—befitting Mallarmé's reputation for difficulty—bear a time gap between the first and second translations? Here is the odd thing, the ultimate surprise: for in the latter, Mallarmé simply brings about the blatant and unapologetic omission of the third of Tennyson's stanzas, significantly *the only one invoking the presence of daylight*. In Tennyson's third stanza, beginning, "Upon the middle of the night . . . ," Mariana says, for the only time, "The day is dreary . . ." to announce the refrain: "He cometh not . . . I would that I were dead." What might Mallarmé's omission point to, in his reworking of his original translation? Might we try, in such a particular case, to find a cause for the omission? And might there be one or a series of hinge words as a syllepsis, having two meanings and thus the clue to something else, perhaps to the retranslation?

What seems most striking in both versions of the translation, and in the original, is the stress in the French versions, as in the English, on the expressions, and from the beginning to the end, on the natural waning of the day, each of which connotes a crucial lean toward death: "The rusted nails fell . . ." and the translation: "Les clous rouillés tombaient . . ."; so that the initial reference in the translation to a tomb (as the French verb *tomber*)—a syllepsis and an overdetermination in anyone's terms—is carried throughout the poem: "Ses larmes tombèrent . . . ses larmes tombaient . . . L'ombre tomba . . . le rayon . . . gisait . . . le jour pencha . . ."— rendering the English "Her tears fell . . . the shadow . . . fell . . . sunbeam lay athwart . . . day was sloping."

One of the more remarkable changes from the first to the second version of the translation occurs in the fourth stanza of the second version, recasting the fifth stanza of the first version to emphasize the tomb, as clearly as does the omission/suppression of the daylight in the stanza left out. We see, to our surprise, in the retranslation, an exclamation point added by Mallarmé that appeared neither in the initial translation nor in Tennyson's poem, and that sets off the drama of the situation as clearly as does the theatrical curtain that frames the scene: "Et toujours, quand baissa la lune et que les vents aigus se levèrent haut et loin, dans le rideau blanc elle vit d'ici à là l'ombre secouée se balancer. Mais quand la lune fut très-bas et les sauvages vents, liés dans leur prison, l'ombre du peuplier tomba sur le lit, par-dessus son front!" There could scarcely be a clearer reference by the tomb in the "tomba" to the gloomy nature of the poem itself than the echo of "ombre . . . tomba . . ." with its final exclamation: after the "front"!

Now the reader may be reminded of a painting from a year almost exactly equidistant from the 1830s in which "Mariana" was written and 1874, in which Mallarmé first translated it: Millais's great painting of 1851 called *Mariana* shows a table set up as a kind of altar with stained-glass windows, like a *table de toilette* for the lovely girl, with several fallen leaves upon it and scattered on the floor. So the exterior has penetrated to the interior, like nature coming in, but only through the artificially colored glass. Across the floor a mouse is scuttling, referring back to the setting of the moated grange. The painting is divided into two parts, with a darker right half, windowless and with a smaller version of the table, with a religious triptych and lighted candles on it and a sort of votive light hanging over it,

FIGURE 2. Sir John Everett Millais, *Mariana* (1851). Oil on panel, 59.7 x 49.5 cm. Based on Shakespeare's character in *Measure for Measure*. Photograph © Tate Gallery, London / Art Resource, New York.

marking yet another prayerful wish. Into this gloom, a perfect rendering of Mariana's own tired waiting, only the tip of her right elbow penetrates, as she makes her remarkable and drastic backward lean, as if exhausted, her hands on her waist and her head thrown back in a wearied position. And that *lean* itself is the key to our visual/verbal reading of this second form of the translation. It perfectly fits Harold Bloom's definition of the lean or the swerve that he terms the *clinamen*: "There is always and only bias, inclination, pre-judgment, swerve . . ." (9). This accentuated backward lean is, in my view, exactly what Mallarmé's rendering picks up most noticeably from the English, together with the quite extraordinary airlessness of the painting (the same suffocating closed-in feeling oppresses the viewer in Rossetti's painting of Mariana), to organize the poem around in his retranslation of sixteen years later than his initial one in *La Dernière Mode*. For in this version, devoted to gloom like the right-hand side of the Millais painting, daylight would not fit. So the day and the light are simply shut out. Such is the power of a (re)translation. Mariana as a name, Mariana as a painting, Mariana as a poem and two translations--all come together in a miraculous coherence now, in 1890, two years before Tennyson's death and Mallarmé's moving elegy: "Tennyson, Seen from Here."

As for the usual question: Why that poem? Radically opposed to the response offered by the first editors about Mallarmé's rush to get out his next issue of the magazine, it seems to this observer that Mariana finds her appropriate place in this ladies' magazine, much of which is about costume and feminine finery: she fits the pattern perfectly. She is clothed, as Godiva is not, but they both have a mane of hair curlier than that of Mallarmé, as curly as Tennyson's own, the poet in drag. Tennyson's third stanza, the one Mallarmé cuts out in his later translation, is significantly the only one in which "the day" figures in the original, where the refrain reads from "my life" in the first stanza to myself ("I am") in the last, and from night to day: "My life . . . The night . . . The day . . . My life . . . The night . . . My life . . . I am." Mallarmé cared immensely about the sound of language: the harmony of being depended on the unity and unison that poetry could bring about. (He was delighted to think, upon his finding of the word "ptyx," which was to rhyme with other sounds in his "allegorical sonnet of itself," that it was a pure invention of his poetry, and not something he might come across elsewhere, as he writes to the famed Egyptologist Lefébure on May 3, 1868: "I've been assured that it doesn't exist in any language, which I'd surely prefer so as to have the delight of creating it through the magic rhyme" [*Selected Letters* 274].)

Concerned so about words, Mallarmé was crucially bothered when they were inappropriate in their sounding—the major example being his concern with how "le jour" projects a sonority longer, richer, and rounder than that of the night, "la nuit," in all its brightness of the *i* vowel: "à côté d'*ombre*, opaque, *ténèbres* se fonce peu: quelle déception, devant la perversité conférant à *jour* comme à *nuit*, contradictoirement, des timbres obscur ici, là clair" ("Beside darkness, opaque, 'shadows' is not very deep; what a disappointment, as to the perversity that confers on 'jour' as on 'nuit,' in contradiction, bright sounds on the latter and dark sounds on the former") ("Crise de vers," *Oeuvres* [1945] 360–68). Or as Bonnefoy phrases it: "For, united with others like it . . . the sound *nuit* will allow many notions to light up reciprocally with reflections come from some other . . . this coming together brought about under a clear sign . . . in the lucidity of pure sound" ("La Poétique" 15). Far from disturbing, this continuing night harmonizes sound and sense in the refrain of Mallarmé's "Mariana": "Ma vie . . . La nuit . . . Ma vie . . . La nuit . . . Ma vie . . . Je suis."

"Je suis." The words all rhyme, as does Tennyson's "my life is dreary . . . I am aweary, aweary," and indeed the poem rendered by Mallarmé works wonderfully, with the same progression from "he isn't coming" (which Mallarmé, however, varies from Tennyson's invariable "he cometh not" to "il ne vient point" [stanza 1]; "il ne vient jamais" [stanza 3]; "il ne vient pas" [stanzas 2, 4, 5]) to "he will not come" ("il ne viendra pas"). Perhaps the most noticeable difference between the two poems is the ellipsis of death in the last stanza: "oh! Dieu!" ends Mariana's exclamation, in which the death wish is totally absorbed and has no need to be reiterated after its preceding strikes. The so-hated day is, in Mallarmé's revision, suppressed from or repressed in the stressed position in the third stanza by the draconian measure (*Measure for Measure* being, as we remember, the source for the poem's "moated grange") of simply removing the stanza! When it is allowed to enter the poem, it is judiciously, if not "faithfully," placed. First, it is innocuous and clichéd in its initial position in his fifth or next-to-last stanza, the *pénultième* (to use one of

Mallarmé's favorite expressions): "all day" / "tout le jour." Why not? This is no "day," this is just part of a temporal sequence. Then comes the whammy: for in the last stanza, in that loathed hour when the sun breaks in, like a spying eye, that hour is already seen, by Mallarmé, as dying, before the day slopes or leans to the west. For Tennyson, the sunbeam just "lay"—was simply lying there, with no indication of slope until the next verse:

> . . . but most she loathed the hour
> When the thick-moted sunbeam lay
> Athwart the chambers, and the day
> Was sloping toward his western bower.

(Tennyson, I, 209)

It is clear how masculine is the day, and how the mystery pertains to the somewhat mysterious Mariana. Now in his version of "Mariana," Mallarmé uses a peculiar verb, applying it to the male sunbeam ("le rayon de soleil"), one that in French has a deadly note to it, for it can only mean to lie down dying or dead: "le rayon de soleil *gisait* au travers des chambres, quand le jour pencha vers le bosquet occidental." So death has entered, quite naturally ("Nature exists, and cannot be added to . . .") (*Prose* 37) right next to the day, leaning to the west in its Mariana-like weariness, and thus needs no repetition in the person of Mariana, who weeps her fatigue, exclaims "oh! Dieu," and there ends the translation—this self-translation, as Mehlman and psychoanalysis would have it (103). Furthermore, the verb *gisait* here acts as the syllepsis that Riffaterre considers crucial to the recognition of the interdependence of intertext and text. And so, it is the very entrance of the sunbeam that spells death to the dream. No need to spell it out again at the end, where the drama has its own power, cutting short the verbal expression, as the day is first cut out, and then cut short; made into a prose statue, a "gisant: ci-gît . . ." ("here lies . . ."). Here in the Mallarmé rendering, itself a poem, lies the day, cut short, felled . . . after a long waiting. No, he didn't come. It is a fitting tomb. We know that the prose poem often emphasizes the edges—beginnings and ends—in order to set itself off as a separate unit: so, in Mallarmé's translation, the extremity of death and the exclamation work to round off the poem, as in the Tennyson original, but with a still more drastic atmosphere.

Yet we could make a case for there being, in the concision of Mallarmé's retranslation with its deliberate literary crime against Tennyson's original, "A salvation, precisely on both sides" (*Oeuvres* [1945] 382; *Prose* 46). For Mallarmé's elegy to Tennyson, "Tennyson, vu d'ici" ("Tennyson, Seen from Here")—a prose piece equivalent to his celebrated verse *Tombeaux* for Poe, Baudelaire, and Verlaine—concludes with a double homage to the two Anglophone poets he revered: Poe and Tennyson. Referring to a "column of the temple called Poetry," he writes of Tennyson: "Let his shade be received there in the very terms of affectionate hyperbole that in his youth, illustrious but still future, Poe addressed him: 'the most noble poetic soul who ever existed' " (*Prose* 73).

In her "Mallarmé and the Bounds of Translation," Rosemary Lloyd points out the difference between the literal "prosaic and lowly function of spelling out the name" described in Mallarmé's "Ballets," in that the name is "stated and not evoked," and the mystery of every naming evocation that remains crucial to the act of poetry (*Prose* 23). In his homage to the poet Théophile Gautier, Mallarmé salutes the "final tremor" in that poet's voice, as it awakens "for the Rose and the Lily the mystery of a name" ("éveille / Pour la Rose et le Lys le mystère d'un nom") (*Oeuvres* [1945] 55). That the "name" and the "noun" share in the meaning of the French "nom" doubles the significance of this mysterious quality of nonliterality, of creation as appellation. Mallarmé's view of Gautier, Poe, and Tennyson in his poetry and prose was the very opposite of spying: it was and remains a vision sufficiently powerful to share, sufficiently discreet to reveal both poet and poem without piercing the curtain of mystery—whether created by curls, ringlets, or straight lines—as all the noble stuff of poetry itself envelops every horse of a genuinely poetic rider.

BLOOMSBURY

Now as for Mallarmé's own highly difficult poems, Roger Fry—the art critic and lecturer, the former lover of Vanessa Bell—was the first to put them into readable English. Fry loved Mallarmé the way many of us love Virginia Woolf, or then Roger Fry himself. It seems he never traveled without a volume of Mallarmé's poems. And, indeed, much of his life and energy, when we look back at them now, seem to have been devoted to his translations and interpretations of Mallarmé, in which his friend Charles Mauron was to be his lifelong companion and collaborator.

Yet some of the problems of Fry's translations of Mallarmé, the great poet of suggestion and understatement, have to do with fidelity itself. How can one be faithful to understatement? Mauron's strange ability to capture that of Virginia Woolf, in his translation of the central part of *To the Lighthouse* and *Orlando*, could be taken as a model of just that fidelity. Fry, in his laudable attempt to remain close to the poet's verbal sequence and to echo his rhythm, often falls flat. However, his collaborations with Julian Bell, Virginia Woolf, and Charles Mauron were wonderfully satisfying to him.

He was understandably delighted that André Gide liked his renderings of Mallarmé and had not excelled him in interpreting that supreme and supremely French poet. In fact, wrote Fry in a letter to his beloved Vanessa Bell on September 5, 1918, Gide had admitted to him that "he hadn't gotten so far as some of us in unravelling the intricate mysteries of his meanings" (*Letters* II: 432). This is already to say, of course, that Fry's famous "formalism" had finally another side to it, slanted toward a willingness, indeed a desire, to tangle with the more mysterious order: the one that signifies. In an odd incident, Fry's Mallarmé translations were stolen in the Avignon train station, so that he and Mauron had to reconstruct them in their entirety. This is yet another testimony to his energy. They were finally completed at Royat (Puy-de-Dôme) on June 26, 1933, only a year before his death.

Mauron wrote an interpretation to go along with Fry's translations, which Fry worked at hard, sometimes with Julian Bell. In Fry's rendering of the anything but literal Mallarmé, he is often very literal and sometimes not remarkably sensitive to the understatements and ambiguities of the French. Occasionally, in fact, I am reminded of Whistler's reactions to Mallarmé's too clear presentation of his deliberate ambiguities—what an irony, given the reputation of the translator, the master of mystery. That said, some of Fry's efforts are as satisfactory as any translation of Mallarmé's suggestiveness can be. One of the best, I think, is of an early poem, "Apparition," which Maurice Denis had illustrated:

La lune s'attristait. Des séraphins en pleurs
Rêvant, l'archet aux doigts, dans le calme des fleurs
Vaporeuses, tiraient de mourantes violes
De blancs sanglots glissant sur l'azur des corolles.
—C'était le jour béni de ton premier baiser.
Ma songerie aimant à me martyriser
S'enivrait savamment du parfum de tristesse
Que même sans regret et sans déboire laisse
La cueillaison d'un Rêve au coeur qui l'a cueilli.
J'errais donc, l'oeil rivé sur le pavé vieilli
Quand avec du soleil aux cheveux, dans la rue
Et dans le soir, tu m'es en riant apparue
Et j'ai cru voir la fée au chapeau de clarté
Qui jadis sur mes beaux sommeils d'enfant gâté
Passait, laissant toujours de ses mains mal fermées
Neiger de blancs bouquets d'étoiles parfumeés.

&

The moon was saddening. Seraphim in tears
Dreaming, bow in hand, in the calm of vaporous
Flowers, were drawing from dying violins
White sobs gliding down blue corollas.
—It was the blessed day of your first kiss.
My dreaming loving to torment me
Was drinking deep of the perfume of sadness
That even without regret and deception is left
By the gathering of a Dream in the heart which has gathered it.
I wandered then, my eyes on the worn pavement
When with the sun in your hair, and in the street
In the evening, you in laughter appeared to me
And I thought I saw the fairy with her cap of brightness
Who once on the beauty sleeps of my spoilt childhood
Passed, letting always her half-closed hands
Snow down white bouquets of perfumed stars.
(*Selected Poetry* 4–5)

We cannot help but admire the way in which some imperfect tenses, "s'attristait" and "s'enivrait," are rendered also in the imperfect, respectively, as "was saddening" and "was drinking," in juxtaposition and alliteration with the "seraphim" and "deep"; whereas two other imperfects, "j'errais donc" and "passait," are rendered by the perfect tense: "I wandered then" and "passed"—the first because the imperfect would have been too heavy with the "then"; the second because "was passing" next to "letting" would have been equally heavy.

Even when Fry is more literal than we might like, he is only rarely heavy-handed. Sometimes his verbal power of ellipsis and allusive elusiveness go past any other efforts I know for the translation of Mallarmé in English: as an example, take his "deep" for "savamment"; his omission of the adjective in "oeil rivé sur" rendered simply and quite sufficiently as "my eyes on" and of the preposition in "laissant toujours de ses mains" as "letting always her . . . hands snow down." Furthermore, "in laughter" for "en riant" seems to catch an epiphanic moment wonderfully, and the use of the passive "is left" for the active French "laisse" at once permits him to keep the word order, with the leaving precisely as the line leaves off and the gathering precisely gathered in the longest line of them all. When Fry is good, he is very, very good.

Fry was greatly relieved at the pertinence of Mauron's commentaries on the poet: "Now I can write my preface to Mallarmé because Mauron completes the edifice," he said (*Selected Letters* 580). It was the sturdy and yet slightly mysterious Julian Bell who helped Charles Mauron with the publication of the Mallarmé, looking over the translations, adding notes and the like, before Leonard and Virginia Woolf's Hogarth Press published the Mallarmé volume, finally, in 1936, after Fry's death, edited by Julian Bell and Charles Mauron, including the latter's commentaries. (They were also published in his *Mallarmé l'obscur*, begun in 1938.)

These remarks, often related to music and to a musical "system of transitions," are illuminating both of Mallarmé's and of Fry's—and Mauron's—enthusiasm for relations between the elements of art: not just formalist, but including that approach, joining meaning and sound. (Fry wrote at least two chapters of a projected book on music.) "The spirit lives by finding relations," writes Mauron (Caws and Wright 566), taking his delight in that sense of relations. His enthusiasm has the same seriousness as that of Roger Fry and is particularly valuable in relation to Fry's flatness. This is from his commentary on "Her pure nails" ("Ses purs ongles"):

But the spirit demands a sense in what it reads; and not, as certain modern poets would have us believe, merely from a prosaic and vulgar preoccupation, but because the spirit lives by finding relations and finds its delight therein, so that to deprive one's phrases of sense is to renounce the richest system of relations that language has created. Mallarmé never neglected such opportunities. He refuses no means of interrelating the words of his poem, on the contrary he combines them all and complicates them, adding to the ties of primary significance a whole network of harmonic suggestions and interweaving the analogies of sound with the analogies of sense. (Mallarmé, *Poems* 14)

According to Fry, Mallarmé's method was to break the theme into pieces, then to reconstruct it, in a cubist fashion, not according to experiential relations, but to pure poetical ones. To Vanessa Bell on June 20, 1933, he maintained the greatness of Mallarmé, "certainly almost the purest poet that ever was in the same sort of way as Cézanne was, in the end, the purest of painters" (Fry, unpublished letters). Whatever hesitations are conveyed by the "certainly almost" contrast, the recurrence of the notion of purity is clearly significant for Roger Fry himself, in all his disinterested intensity. Whatever a present reader may think of the literal edifice constructed by Roger Fry, it would be small-minded in the extreme not to appreciate his sustained effort in constructing it. His unchallenged stature as a critic and his enthusiasm for all his projects easily outweigh any hesitation we might have over his results; they are symptomatic of the period in which he did them.

It was, after all, Fry's particular radiance that situated the modernism of Bloomsbury in what I think was its truest light: the light of France and French art. This direction of influence balanced Mallarmé's rendering of Whistlerian early modernism, albeit via a Japanese perspective, for the French. All these minds connect, in Bloomsbury and in France: for, from the beginning, Vanessa Bell loved Whistler's work; Roger Fry loved Vanessa and, finally, also Whistler's work, although he began by Cézanne worship; more importantly, he translated Mallarmé, over and over, for far more than twenty years.

And then, reminiscent of the odd loss of Mallarmé's original essay "Manet and the Impressionists," Roger Fry's translations were lost to a thief in the Avignon train station or then in the Gare St.-Lazare, as Mauron tells it (Caws and Wright 365). He had to wait for them to rise from the dead, as he thought of it: destruction turned out to be his Beatrice too. For rise they did, and as Julian Bell rather elliptically described it, one piece came in from here, one from there. . . . So Fry picked up the pieces and enlisted the commentaries of Charles Mauron, the ex-chemist and translator of Forster, T. E. Lawrence, Virginia Woolf, and Henry James. Mauron, losing his eyesight, was urged by Fry to take on the task of commenting on Mallarmé in Fry's translations and was repeatedly suggested by Fry—sometimes with success—as a translator of works from English, which he knew perfectly. Thus it was that he translated a chapter of *Orlando*, two Henry James stories, and the novels of Forster. This work on Mallarmé prepared the way for Mauron's later work on Mallarmé, significant in the development of his method, *la psychocritique*, or psycho-criticism.

What Roger Fry had cared about so much was finished, at his death, by Mauron with Julian Bell before the latter went off to get himself killed in the Spanish civil war, against the advice of Mauron, whom he trusted, and the wishes of Vanessa. Another loss.

But what we have, besides the rather literalizing translations, is the elaborate correspondence around the layers of Mallarmé's possible meanings and their truly obsessive hold on Fry as on Mauron. Nothing had held Fry like this: we have tale after tale of his cycling off to sketch some cathedral in the early morning, guiding the others through obscure byways later in the day to see some little-known piece of art, wearing everyone out until midnight, and then exclaiming how he and Julian had just enough time to play a game of chess and translate another sonnet. Then he would lie on his camp bed, reading for hours, until he sprang up before breakfast to bike off to some other church. He put me to shame, said Clive Bell, far younger: Look at him!

Roger Fry's immense generosity of spirit meant he had everything to give to what he loved, and you can feel that in his own poems, in his translations of Rimbaud, Baudelaire, and particularly Mallarmé. I have been poring over the manuscripts of those and marveling now at their precision. I used to reject their literality, preferring suggestion to statement as I thought Mallarmé would. Yet now I see Fry's mind at work, seeing just how the same sorts of things we lament, and he sometimes lamented in his painting—the static quality, the lack of emotion—show through in his translations, even as his musical ear is just. Let me give an example of that precision, that justness from *Hérodiade*: trying out equivalents for "seul," he tries "solitary," then "lonely," and ends up with "lone." That seems to me just right, like the less ordinary "fierceness" chosen over "ferocity"; for "décroître," he tries "ungrow," then opts for "grow less," and "aether" before settling on "azure." If God is anywhere in the details, it is certainly in such translations.

As for Fry's remarks on Mallarmé's style, among the more useful seem to me his distinction between the poetical and the witty effects of language: that in wit, the vibrations come to a stop, whereas in poetry like that of Mallarmé, the vibrations continue, as in the Chinese sense of "stop-short"—unlike an epigram, in poetry the words stop short, but the sense goes on. In our age so still influenced by Walter Benjamin's analysis of the "aura" of the object, Fry's study of just how Mallarmé uses the cumulative effect of the auras of words is all the more striking.

It was always a labor of self-abnegation, for Mallarmé knew how to listen: "the poet's voice must be stilled and the initiative taken by the words themselves . . . as they meet in unequal collision." Now I want to latch on to that last adjective, which sticks in my mind: "unequal." Thinking of that inequality, I think also of his celebrated statement, here translated by Rosemary Lloyd: "I believe that when lines are so perfectly delimited, what we should aim for above all, in a poem, is that the words—which are already sufficiently individual not to receive external impressions—*reflect upon each other to the point of appearing not to have their own color anymore, but to be merely transitions within an entire gamut* . . ." (letter to François Coppée, December 5, 1866; *Selected Letters* 69). Reciprocal relations within the text form a primary component of interior shaping.

At the death of Roger Fry in 1934, Charles Mauron wrote a series of eighteen sonnets dedicated to him: *Esquisses pour le Tombeau d'un Peintre* (Sketches for the tomb of a painter), in his *Poèmes Français et Provençaux: Evocations* (French and Provencal poems: Evocations). The last sonnet begins:

Tu ne reviendras pas . . .

&

You won't come back again . . .

And ends:

> Mais je puis te chercher toujours. Mort sage, entends,
> Tous mes jours, chaque jour. Sache-le, du moins: tant
> Que, rumeurs devinées de l'une à l'autre rive,
>
> Ton absence et ton chant, partout et nulle part,
> A leurs chuchotements lieront l'âme attentive,
> Un creux tombeau bruira de ton murmure épars.
> (*Poèmes* 78)

&

> But I can seek you still. Dead wise one, listen,
> All my days, every one. Know this, at least: as long as
> Sounds are even slightly heard from one shore to the next
>
> Your absence and your song, everywhere and nowhere,
> To their whispers will tie the attentive soul,
> A hollow tomb will resound with your slight murmur.

Mauron never stopped developing his thoughts about Mallarmé. In 1938 he prepared *Mallarmé l'obscur*, which appeared only two years later, picking up some of the ideas he had first expressed in the work with Fry, as he explains in the two prefaces to the work, the first in 1939, the second in 1941. The work consists of a hundred-page discussion of the great poet's difficulty—in which he suggests that the next volume after "obscurity" might be devoted to "illumination"—followed by careful commentaries on many of Mallarmé's poems, some rephrased after the initial ones done for the New Directions volume.

Mallarmé's reputation for obscurity was certainly enhanced by the lecture given at Oxford and Cambridge, "La Musique et les lettres" (*Prose* 31–45). He would have liked to have lectured in London also, as Charles Mauron did on one of his two visits to England, the first under the aegis of Roger Fry and the next under that of Margery Fry and E. M. Forster. Discouraged by the sight of his audience, Mallarmé was well aware of the little contact he had with them. But it is, appropriately enough, to this lecture that Mauron refers the most frequently in his discussion of the net or constellation of relations between images whose association explains, time after time, the so-called "obscurities" of the texts (Mallarmé, *Poems* 14). His use of the term "constellations" shows his spirit imbued with the Mallarmean metaphoric. These "obsessive metaphors"—such as the lost Eden and his own impotence, the series of absences, or, later, the association between the wing, the fan, and the veil ("aile," "éventail," "voile")—are based as surely on their musical harmony; thus the wonderfully obsessive references in "La Musique et les lettres." Mauron, himself a musician, was given a piano by his good friend Forster and, in his increasing blindness, resorted to scores in Braille. The keyboard to which he felt so close provided him with the further elaboration of the all-important metaphor of the system of passages from one key to another (Mallarmé, *Poems* 74). Translation is just another system of passages.

Mauron, fascinated by the title of *The Meaning of Meaning: A Study of the Influence of Language upon Thought and the Science of Symbolism* (the book by Charles Ogden and I. A. Richards, whose title he translates as *Que signifie "signifie"?*), continues to insist on the interpretability of Mallarmé's meanings, provided the interpretation of such a poet's life and work is both exterior, concerned with the life, and interior, as in this metaphoric analysis of the work, a model of mental courage. "If he often seems obscure to us," writes Mauron, "I mean if our mind does not go where his went, that is because he dared to take the leap, whereas we are afraid" (Mallarmé, *Poems* 78). Where Mallarmé leapt, Mauron suggests here and elsewhere, is into a kind of nothing that is both positive and negative, like the nothing at the center of the philosophy of the Tao—clearly stated in his essay on "Mallarmé and the Tao." It is that nothing that will lead to something crucial linking Mallarmé's work, and Mauron's interpretation, to Virginia Woolf's rewriting of the obsession.

Mauron's version of Mallarmé's losses is a powerful one. So the deaths of his beloved sister Maria and of his son Anatole mark the conjunction between life and text. As for Mauron himself, he knew, in another sense, what loss was—for after an explosion in the chemical factory where he worked, his sight was constantly threatened. It was Roger Fry who persuaded his friend E. M. Forster to take on the impoverished Mauron as a translator; Fry who persuaded Forster to make possible a voyage in which Mauron could capture in his mind forever the sight of great Italian paintings, to look over when he could no longer see; and who then himself understood it would be better for Mauron to go to one of the *décades* at Pontigny on humanism, to meet the persons in charge of translations for Plon in Paris. So it was through Roger Fry that Charles Mauron was able to recuperate some strength during his loss, physical and psychic.

Charles and Marie Mauron were often Roger's own strength in France, when he most needed it—for instance, at the time of his loss of his Breton mistress Josette Coatmellec. Thinking an African statue whose picture he sent her was a mocking signal, and that he took their relationship trivially, she had stood dramatically on the cliffs of Le Havre, looking toward England, the land of her lover, and shot herself. Roger wrote her biography, so far unpublished, and wrote many poems to her in French. To the Maurons he could lament his loss. He was very close to the couple, even sharing a house with them in St. Rémy, parking his bike there, near the high cliffs of Les Baux where they had all met.

Mauron's psychocritical method remains of interest even now. To sum it up, from his own *Introduction à la psychocritique* (Introduction to psychocriticism), the subtitle of his *Des Métaphores obsédantes au mythe personnel* (From obsessive metaphors to personal myth) (32), you superimpose various texts of the same author like Galton photographs atop each other, and groups of images or associations appear, probably involuntary ones, which you then look for through the work in their repetitive structures, usually dramatic, forming a personal myth of the unconscious personality and its evolution, to be compared with the writer's life. What he did for Mallarmé, he did of course long after Roger Fry's death. But it was their work together on the Mallarmé poems that led to Mauron's intense involvement with Mallarmé, at the source of his method.

I want simply to notice something about the group of these figures meeting in my superposition here and in the following chapter on Woolf. Fry is fascinated by Mauron's interpretation of Mallarmé—and, in a sort of Girardian triangle, by Mauron himself. Virginia Woolf is alternately bemused by Fry's fascination with Mauron—

that blind Frenchman, as she calls him—and herself impressed with his erudition. After Roger's and Julian's deaths, she writes Mauron to say he understood Roger better than anyone, and that in her view he was by far the most interesting French critic (unpublished letter to Charles Mauron). And after Julian's death, her sister Vanessa, as Julian and Roger had done, takes comfort and psychological refuge in visiting the Maurons at St. Rémy. It was not just Mallarmé whom Mauron understood so well, but Roger and Julian also.

It was something, I think, about loss. For Charles Mauron's analysis of Mallarmé's personal myth, relating to the double deaths of his sister and son, may suggest a way of considering Fry's fascination with Mallarmé, amply demonstrated. Having lost his wife to madness and Vanessa to Duncan Grant, and then having on his mind the suicide of his mistress Josette Coatmellec, Roger had his own losses. As did Virginia Woolf, whose masterpiece *The Waves* laments, celebrates, and centers around the absence and loss of her dead brother Thoby. So Mauron's analysis of death or nothingness as the obsessive metaphor holding together Mallarmé's work is seen to work for Virginia Woolf and Roger Fry too, even as Mauron himself, losing his outward sight, gained an insight that holds true beyond his own consciousness, determining an inner shape to his reflections.

If the compensations for loss differ widely, in life and work, our kinds of fascination and their images often converge. Many of us are haunted, like Mauron, by Mallarmé's obsession with nothingness, the absence at the center of it all. Let me just muster the fewest of examples that came to me when I was preparing the New Directions volume of Mallarmé translations, the prime case being "nul ptyx," the negative phrase containing that word he had hoped would not be found anywhere, so that it would be pure invention, reflecting on all sides. This nullity was an undoing, "abolishing" any triviality, no matter how precious, like "Une dentelle s'abolit" (*Selected Poems* 58–59), and like Virginia Woolf's favorite phrase of Mallarmé, taken from her reading of "Crise de vers" and signaled in her *Reading Notebooks*: "Abolie, la prétention, esthétiquement une erreur, quoiqu'elle régit les chefs-d'oeuvre, d'inclure au papier subtil du volume autre chose que par exemple l'horreur de la forêt, ou le tonnerre muet épars au feuillage; non le bois intrinsèque et dense des arbres." (Roughly translatable as "Annulled, that claim, aesthetically an error, although it is taken as a rule by masterpieces, including in the subtle paper of the volume anything else than, for example, the horror of the forest, or the silent thunder scattered through the foliage; not the dense wood intrinsic in the trees"; 193). The blank mirror of Igitur plays the same role, undoing anything that would have taken itself seriously. . . .

More null and void than even such a "nul ptyx" is this nothing of "Salut" ("Toast"):

> Rien, cette écume, vierge vers
> A ne désigner que la coupe
> ❧
>
> Nothing, this foam, virgin verse
> Showing nothing but the cup
> (*Selected Poems* 3; my retranslation)

Or of "Brise marine" ("Sea Breeze"):

> Rien, ni les vieux jardins reflétés par les yeux
> ❧
>
> Nothing, not the old gardens reflected in those eyes
> (*Selected Poems* 16–17; my retranslation)

How, the translator often says to herself, to translate nothing? Mallarmé's circling around a center where nothing holds can be seen as a negative obsession, or one that leads to a masterpiece, so seen as both negative and positive, Zen-style, in the "disparition élocutoire du poète / the speaking disappearance of the poet" (Terry 264–73).

Translating Mallarmé is sometimes like an intense meditation, and sometimes its bare image. It is solitude itself, working late in an empty study with some yet other *nul* and nil and nothing staring at you from every mirroring wall with nary anybody to accompany your very uncertain vigil over what turns out to be, every time at its best, *rien*. And this is exactly what one plunges into: the kind of lake or trap that looking turns out to be: *lacs* fits both senses. Mallarmé's great early poem "Le Pitre châtié" ("The Chastised Clown") illustrates, from its beginning in the difficult final version, how this works. Piercing the circus wall, the performer/poet leaps—as with a virgin or initial gesture—into the water or trap, thereby washing off the cosmetic paint that was, in fact, his self. His chastisement is his loss of his painted self, perhaps the true one.

The first version of the poem was far less arduous. Instead of the impossible beginning with the more than awkward to pronounce or perform as an initial exclamation "Yeux," there was the more melodious "Pour ses yeux,—pour nager dans ces lacs . . ." As before, I want to stress the importance of the poem's beginning and conclusion.

Pour ses yeux,—pour nager dans ces lacs, dont les quais
Sont plantés de beaux cils qu'un matin bleu pénètre,
J'ai, Muse,—moi, ton pitre,—enjambé la fenêtre
Et fui notre baraque où fument tes quinquets.

Et d'herbes enivré, j'ai plongé comme un traître
Dans ces lacs défendus, et, quand tu m'appelais,
Baigné mes membres nus dans l'onde aux blancs galets,
Oubliant mon habit de pitre au tronc d'un hêtre.

Le soleil du matin séchait mon corps nouveau.
Et je sentais fraîchir loin de ta tyrannie
La neige des glaciers dans ma chair assainie,

Ne sachant pas, hélas! quand s'en allait sur l'eau
Le suif de mes cheveux et le fard de ma peau,
Muse, que cette crasse était tout le génie!
(*Oeuvres* [1998] 150)

❧

For her eyes,—to swim in these lakes, whose shores
Are planted with lovely lashes pierced by a blue morning,
I have, Muse,—I, your clown,—stepped across the windowsill
And fled our tent smoking with your flares.

And drunken on grass blades I have dived like a traitor
In these forbidden lakes, and, at your summons,
I've bathed my bare limbs in the water with the white pebbles
Forgetting my clown costume at the trunk of a beech tree.

The morning sun was drying my new body
And I felt cooling far from your tyranny
The snow of glaciers in my healthy flesh,

Not knowing, alas, when the water swept away
The suet of my hair and the makeup of my skin,
Muse, that this stuff was genius itself!

So my translation printed here wants to keep, from the first version,
the clarity, in which all the details are spelled out, and conjunctions
left in: "and . . . and . . . and . . ." It moves slowly, and is meant to.

Whereas, in the translation of the second version, it wants to
stress the sharp veering toward ellipsis, the elision of the obvious.
What the final version brings in most noticeably is the repeated in-
cision of the *y* as in the opening "yeux," and the "y vierge" to the
final "noyé," and then the *v* of "ivresse," évoquais," "innovais," and
"vierge"—cutting, virginal, plunging, melodramatic, erotic: all of
that.

Yeux, lacs avec ma simple ivresse de renaître
Autre que l'histrion qui du geste évoquais
Comme plume la suie ignoble des quinquets,
J'ai troué dans le mur de toile une fenêtre.

De ma jambe et des bras limpide nageur traître,
A bonds multipliés, reniant le mauvais
Hamlet! C'est comme si dans l'onde j'innovais
Mille sépulcres pour y vierge disparaître.

Hilare or de cymbale à des poings irrité,
Tout à coup le soleil frappe la nudité
Qui pure s'exhala de ma fraîcheur de nacre,

Rance nuit de la peau quand sur moi vous passiez,
Ne sachant pas, ingrat! Que c'était tout mon sacre,
Ce fard noyé dans l'eau perfide des glaciers.
(*Oeuvres* [1998] 348)
❧

Eyes, lakes with my simple passion to be reborn
Other than the actor, evoking with gestures
For feather the ugly soot of stage lights,
I have pierced a window in the canvas wall.

Clear traitor swimmer, with my legs and arms
Leaping and bounding, denying the wrong
Hamlet! As if I created in the waves
A thousand tombs in which to virgin disappear.

Joyous gold of the cymbal fists have inflamed,
Suddenly the sun strikes the barrenness pure
Exhaled from my coolness like mother-of-pearl

Stale night of the skin when you swept over me,
Ungrateful! Ignorant of my whole consecration,
That grease paint drowned in faithless glacier water.
(*Selected Poetry* 5–7)

Now from the second version, the English can only with a certain
awkwardness retain the cutting edge. Robert Greer Cohn, the great
Mallarmé expert, offers the following version, in a commented translation, where the ambiguities are spelled out:

> . . . it's as if in the wave I innovated [created]
> Countless tombs in which to disappear [a] virgin.
> (*Toward the Poems* 235)

Another of his interesting moves is to insist on the verb "slap" for
"frappe"—instead of the more everyday and obvious "strike," which
I used, thinking of a sunstroke. . . .

In any case, to work on the nullity and the disappearance of the
actor and the self is admittedly of course only a pale imitation of Mallarmé mirroring himself in *Igitur*, staring always at the self and vacancy, as Yves Bonnefoy points out in his "Igitur ou le photographe."
But I want for a moment to think about this in relation to Virginia
Woolf's own haunting by mirrors and, like Mallarmé, by Hamlet.
The hesitating Hamlet personality always tries to see, stare at, and
seize what the self might be, in all its parts, like some play with mir-

rors, like Woolf's own last piece, the unsettling *Between the Acts*. As the audience holds mirrors up to their faces, they reflect her own certain and uncertain way of multiplying being to overcome loss.

There may be for her no Shakespeare, but there is, as there was for Mallarmé, the always present figure of the hesitater Hamlet, that latent lord who could not become. "I reach," writes Virginia Woolf,

> what I might call a philosophy . . . that the whole world is a work of art; that we are parts of the work of art. *Hamlet* or a Beethoven quartet is the truth about this vast mass that we call the world. But there is no Shakespeare, there is no Beethoven; certainly and emphatically there is no God; we are the words; we are the music; we are the thing itself. (*Moments* 72)

What he, Hamlet, hovers over is a whole space in which Mallarmé and Woolf seem often to encounter each other, a space somewhere between symbolism and post-symbolism.

Take something so small and great as Mallarmé's brief text "The White Waterlily," situated at the heart of his *Divagations*, place it next to Woolf's "The Lady in the Looking Glass" and "The Fascination of the Pool," and you find yourself reflecting differently.

In Mallarmé's understated and haunting anecdote or prose poem, the poet/narrator rows his boat out in the heat of a July day to salute a neighboring yet unknown lady whose waterside retreat is "wetly impenetrable" (*Selected Poetry* 65–67). The fact that he has not seen her, upon his setting out, preserves her possibility as only suggestive, keeping the glow of the uncertain: "I evoked her as completely shining"; the fact that he never will glimpse more than this evocation, before returning from his quest, conveys its own fulfillment. Evocation is all that meeting could never be. How deeply Mallarmé.

Perhaps she comes out on her dock; perhaps the rustle he perceives indicates her nearness; perhaps the slight sound he hears is her step receding—who knows? Their almost encounter brings them closer than could any real coming together in any real space: this is, after all, the space of poetry. "Separate as we are, we are together. Now I plunge within this mingled intimacy" (*Selected Poetry* 66–67). And he plucks, like that so celebrated rose absent from all bouquets, her "virgin absence scattered through this solitude," on this occasion the white water lily, swelling with the "exquisite absence of self," which is the proper pursuit of a lady stopping just at the edge of the water. This is the essence of Mallarmé.

And of Virginia Woolf in one of her moods. Like "The White Waterlily," "The Lady in the Looking Glass" and "The Fascination of the Pool," both to be discussed in the next chapter, locate in their play of glass and water, of mind and word, the strange double work of fullest presence and absolute absence. They move tremulously from a clear speculation on reflection itself in different modes—lake, mirror, pool—to a narration that, were it a question of writers less imbued with symbolism, might be expected to lead somewhere. In any other case, it might be fitting to pose such ordinary questions as these: What will the setting out on the lake or the peering into a mirror yield? What shore or vision will the boat lead to? How will the mirror in its changing reflect the stillness of what it reflects? How do the ripples of remembered experience in the pool overlap?

But the expectations instilled in us by previous readings of Mallarmé and Woolf utterly forestall any such expectations. These texts with their baroque over- and undertones perform exactly in the ambiguous reflective mode of the best writings of both: what they do not fix remains desirable and desired. The almost vision by the water is better than any concrete sight or sound, preserving the mobility of the pre- and post-reflection, the purity of the water lily. In "The Lady in the Looking Glass," the unsteady reflection in the glass is mobile until the lady comes back in from her wandering to be frozen by her pile of letters. "The Fascination of the Pool" is made up precisely of all the multiple pasts captured within it, the sounds of all those voices that lose their mysterious lure only when the pool falls still and the house is put up for sale. The placard reflected in its center works like any announcement, it *states*, which is the exact opposite of the symbolist reverberation that is suggestion—the surprise at the very heart of the symbolist experience.

v. *Woolf in Translation*

OBJECT LESSONS

THE OBJECT ITSELF should be a subject of careful witness in whatever language it is addressed, and of this, Virginia Woolf is continually conscious. Considering Woolf's objects as they are rendered into French reveals some strange things about both languages, the original and what happens to it.

"I had my usual visual way of putting it," Woolf writes in *A Sketch of the Past* (118). Often in her works, the very concreteness of the action repeated seems to harden it into a thing, asking, like any visible object, to be dealt with by the mind. Intangible, it is nevertheless handleable, manageable, both words bearing the sense of the original Latin *manus*, or "hand." The moment is objectified. Woolf has, more than most authors, the gift of formulating mere instants into things, nowhere more clearly visible, touching and touchable, than in her sense of her very particular past. As surely as the flowers on her mother's dress in the same text are there for us to touch, we find ourselves in the lap of the author now recalling her first memory, in the lap of her mother. Passage, scene, and object are celebrated:

> I therefore saw the flowers she was wearing very close; and can still
> see purple and red and blue, I think, against the black; they must have
> been anemones, I suppose. (*Sketch* 64)

This initial passage from text-thing to mind has colors and shapes preceding any indication of their meaning. The suspending delay until the final "anemones" works closely with the memory. It is precisely that sort of *delay of the object* that I want to examine. How does such an object manage to enable the imagination? "If I were a painter I should paint these first impressions," Woolf says (66), and we notice that the colors she would now choose are pale yellow, silver, and green—precisely *not* the purple and red and blue of the lap scene. For those were given, not chosen. Crucial to Woolf's sense of dealing with objective and object-laden language is her passion for sight itself.

Among all her texts, it is the celebrated "Mark on the Wall" that provides the most prolonged examination of how the visual relates to the mental. For it is the very undefinition of that mark from the outset until the conclusion that permits the mind to wander in its trace, to wonder about its track. Its wholly ambiguous nature permits the idea to expand, until finally its being is resolved. So the problematic thing is quite often just what provokes the imagination. The most enduring object is the one allowing the mind sufficient room to move about it. I trust the trace of this mark to endure through the rest of my commentary:

> Perhaps it was the middle of January in the present year that I first looked up and saw the mark on the wall. In order to fix a date it is necessary to remember what one saw. . . . How readily our thoughts swarm upon a new object, lifting it a little way, as ants carry a blade of straw so feverishly, and then leave it. . . . ("La Marque," trans. Nordon, 12–14)

And later the obsession returns:

> I must jump up and see for myself what that mark on the wall really is—a nail, a rose-leaf, a crack in the wood? (30)

It is, I think, a matter of keeping the problem of the thing in suspension, of not resolving it too rapidly into the system of understanding. It has to be available over time in its ambiguous freedom for our minds to engage with it.

The precise difficulty of translating this passage stems from the necessity of capturing the obsessive repetition of the verb "looking up." This is actually the point of the story, as the meditation wanders here and there, still anchored to the fixation:

I first looked up . . .
when I looked up . . .
I looked up through . . .
if I got up and looked at it . . .
and if I were to get up . . .
I must jump up and see for myself . . . (12–30)

Pierre Nordon's French rendering of this work manages to retain the looseness of the "perhaps," as well as the determination of the "Yes, it must have been," but loses this witty repeat, attenuating, by the variation of the verb, exactly this crucial repetition. This is precisely what so often happens in the accepted translations of Henry James—when there is too much repetition, the French rendering avoids it and opts for "elegant variation," just when it might signify something urgent, like an obsession:

levant les yeux, j'ai vu . . .
J'ai levé les yeux et j'ai vu . . .
j'observais à travers . . .
je pourrais me lever . . .
et si à la minute je me levais . . .
Il faut que je me tire de mon fauteuil . . . (13–31)

Hélène Bokanowski, in her rendering, keeps more specifically the repetitions:

lorsque levant les yeux, j'aperçus . . .
ayant les yeux levés . . .
je pourrais me lever . . .
mais si je me levais . . .
et si je devais me lever . . .
Il faut absolument que je me lève . . .
("La Marque," trans. Bokanowski, 67–73)

The insistence prevailing in this latter translation, like the one in the English source, stresses the wandering of the imagination around this fixed point.

As for the insistence upon the object, and the anchoring of the imagination to it, if we compare this state of mind with that prevailing at the same time in the European scene, at least the one in France of the 1920s and 1930s, a context for this attitude toward the object comes clear. In the world of the surrealists, and in the mind and writings of their leader, André Breton—whose mind *was* the mind of surrealism—the object in itself was celebrated as potentially imagination-provoking, provided that the imagination could be kept in excitement, in the very suspension that Woolf's "Mark on the Wall" makes its own object.

Take the moment when Breton and Alberto Giacometti are wandering together in the Marché aux Puces, that magic place in which new discoveries were always at hand. They come upon a wooden slipper, in the form of a spoon, or is it a spoon in the form of a slipper? Breton's eroticizing imagination goes to work. From this spoon-slipper, pictured in *Nadja*, there emerges a certain genie of a dream, as from some sort of pipe bubble. Just as from those paper Japanese flowers that surprisingly spring forth upon the immersion of the small folded paper in water, which Proust dwells upon so long, there emerges a universe. Pages later Breton is still delighting in this imaginative windfall arising from this slipper-spoon. So are we. That spoon holds a great deal.

Or take, as a further example of that epoch's imagining, the scene in which Breton, Roger Caillois, and Jacques Lacan are huddled at a table around a Mexican jumping bean. More ink has been spilled over this moment than over many, and for good reason. It is now a matter of knowing who wanted to do what with that bean and its potential: one of the participants at the table scene wanted to open the bean to see why it jumped, one wanted to let the imagination roam unrestricted in its lack of precise understanding, and one of them—the one Breton believed himself to be, then and later—wanted to let them collectively imagine what was going on in the bean and then, only after the imagination had been exhausted, open the little thing. Now the point here is the collective imagination in its freedom to spin itself around the object. For in the world of the surrealists, collective experiments were valued above all else, in the mode of collective games; collective findings, as in the *objet trouvé*, or "found object"; collective drawings and projections, as in the *cadavre exquis*, or "exquisite corpse"—the folded paper on which separate words or separate body parts developed, upon unfolding, into sentences, such as "the exquisite corpse will drink the new wine," or into complete if bizarre bodies. I want to imagine that Woolf's spinning of a world, often from her things, functions between her imagination and that of her readers in much the same way.

Now this joy in putting off the moment of understanding—say, delaying the discovery of just exactly what the little thing that jumps about on the table or the trace of the thing on the wall might be—is illustrated by the three men gathered around the table. (I have sometimes found myself wondering how different it all might have been if one of the surrealizing women artists or writers had been present, or perhaps the surrealist child/woman or woman/fish Mélusine; I rather suspect the deliberation would have taken an alternative course: more patience, more conversation, less macho argument.) The point here is that of the *imaginative delay*, giving space and time for the mind to wander and wonder about the object. It is that sort of delay for which we read Henry James with such delight and that most translators find impossible to convey.

As for that mark on that wall and Woolf's technique in assaying it—assaying as in the French etymology of the *essay*, trying it out, giving it its own story or essay—it is no secret that Alain Robbe-Grillet picked it up in his superbly objectifying, imagination-provoking novel *La Jalousie*. At one of the table scenes, a mark on the wall arouses a long flurry of wonderment: just the kind that appears so long before it, in Virginia Woolf, whose techniques were so elegantly imitated in France.

In any case, the point is the delay, the uncertainty hovering so propitiously about the object. Breton gives the diametrically opposed example in his disquisition against what he thinks of as the realism of Dostoyevsky in his description of a room in *Crime and Punishment*, which he calls a useless or "null" moment. Nothing is going on, in Breton's eyes; nothing is meaningful; nothing is intense. So experience is nullified, rendered dull. We *know* what is going on. Surrealism makes a big point of opposing the "already seen" or "already known": thus Breton's declining to open the jumping bean before a delay sufficient to leave room for the imagination.

Woolf's "moments of being" are all meaningful; none are null. It is often a delay of understanding that extends and intensifies the moment, making space for the mind. What is essential is not to diminish the margin around the object so transforming to the mind, and therefore not to rush its presentation. And this is where the unimaginative translator or editor can cause unimaginable harm. The description of the object needs—to use a term from that great English poet Gerard Manley Hopkins—its *indwelling*.

It might seem that the necessary translation of the object from one language to another would rule against the desirable suspension of belief that imagination calls for. In particular, in the very passion of the French language for clarity, for definition, comes a certain rub. How to retain that imaginative, suspensive glory of the Woolfian undefinition? I am fascinated with (and sometimes discouraged by) the ways in which Virginia Woolf's texts are not only translated into French, but commented upon for students. The overlay of the editor's/translator's judgment is often obnoxious. It is precisely the all-important Woolfian delay that proves unbearable for one of the editors and translators of the bilingual teaching editions of Woolf's stories, as it does, but less obviously, for some other translators.

Take the notes to the bilingual edition of the story called "Solid Objects," titled in Pierre Nordon's translation for the Livre de Poche edition as "Objets tangibles," whereas in Bokanowski's edition, it becomes "Objets massifs." Here, I think without any hesitation that "tangible" is the correct solution, but I understand the other rendering of the title. As furniture can be "massif," even if movable (thus, "meuble," as opposed to "immeuble," immobile), the point of Woolf's objects is that they are significant if infinitely mobile in our minds.

Ah, sadness. For here the bilingual edition prepared by Pierre Nordon reads like any French textbook for the lycée. (The editorial comment on Woolfian technique, when the delay has exasperated the French schoolmaster or -mistress, reads like this, with the editor addressing the young mind, presumably a mind exhausted with Woolfian consideration: "Enfin un nom propre!" ("Finally, a proper name!") The implication is, of course, that Woolf does not conform to the standard (French) way of writing (indeed, she does not).

Later this editor—who has objected to Woolf's rapid-fire delivery at one point and to the delay of intellectual gratification at another— exclaims, about a story he would prefer to see extended, at what he deems the unnecessary abbreviation of the story that it would have more properly occupied more space and time: "le déroulement du récit exigeant une durée plus longue" ("the progression of the tale needing to last longer"[!]) ("Objets tangibles," 62). Clearly, Nordon had not contemplated the readerly imaginative joy at the end of a Jane Austen novel that presents the conclusion—oh, you know, marriage and all that—in shotgun style. "Dear Reader," indeed.

Having glanced at the editorial problem of how this exasperatingly brilliant modernist author is introduced to the general public, I want to look at a few translation moments from a few stories, objectifying them, in fact. As for the story about objects themselves, with its two translated titles, it is from the initial lump of glass so fascinating to the protagonist that an entire story develops: first a character study and then a whole narrative—thus the truly massive importance of the translation of that one word: the "lump." It is one of those cases upon which hangs the talent of the translator and that displays the luck of the language. English is, as often, fortunate here in its ability to lump. We lump together things, knowing just what that means. Here the lump matters all the more, to the development around this centrally significant (and small) lump, large only in its meaning. Tangible or solid: solid gives, like lump, the lumpiness, a kind of stolid approach. Thus, "massif" is possible, but it loses the tangible point: the protagonist touches an idea that becomes a life. So I shall stick to "tangible" for my part. Yet in this case the object endures, which is the point: "si dur, si concentré, si précis . . ." ("so hard, so concentrated, so definite . . .") ("Objets tangibles" 66). They are truly indestructible, Woolf's objects.

Here is the English source and two French translations.

As he was choosing which of these things to make it, still working his fingers in the water, they curled round something hard—a full drop of solid matter—and gradually dislodged a large irregular lump, and brought it to the surface. When the sand coating was wiped off, a green tint appeared. It was a lump of glass, so thick as to be almost opaque. . . . It pleased him; it puzzled him; it was so hard, so concentrated, so definite an object compared with the vague sea and the hazy shore. ("Objets tangibles" 66–68)

Pierre Nordon's translation runs like this:

> Comme il hésitait entre ces différentes appellations, ses doigts qui trituraient dans l'eau entourèrent quelque chose de dur, un fragment massif, et peu à peu extirpèrent et ramenèrent à la surface un gros morceau compact. La couche de sable essuyée, une teinte verte apparut. C'était un morceau de verre, opaque tellement il était épais. . . . Cela plaisait à John, l'intriguait; un object si dur, si concentré, si précis, comparé au flou de la mer et au vaporeux du rivage. (67–69)

The emphasis falls on the bigness of the fragment and on the "gros morceau compact" ("fat compact piece") not simply thick, as in the English, but large and massive: "massif . . . gros . . . épais" ("massive . . . fat . . . thick").

Hélène Bokanowski's translation reads with the play of the fingers more flexible—"faisant jouer" ("making it play") like the fingers working in the English, instead of the heaviness of Nordon's "trituraient" ("rolling it over, manipulating it")—and, above all, the simplicity of the "gros morceau" as just irregular, with the accent falling on the irregularity and not on the "massif," so that the thickness is concentrated but not overwhelming:

> Comme il choisissait entre toutes ces choses tout en faisant jouer ses doigts dans l'eau, ils étreignirent quelque chose de dur—un gros morceau compact—et peu à peu, il ébranla une masse irrégulière, la ramena à la surface. La gangue de sable essuyée, une teinte verte se révéla. C'était un morceau de verre, épais au point d'en être presque opaque. . . . Cela lui plaisait; l'intriguait. C'était un objet si dur, si condensé, si défini, comparé aux vagues de la mer, au flou de la plage. ("Objets massifs" 78–79)

Virginia Woolf calls on every inch of sensitivity one can muster to qualify, dwell on, *translate* each object as it reflects something or someone in the text where it figures. The lump as tangible object concentrates the story of obsession in "Solid Objects." The pencil of "Street Haunting" that the narrator uses as a pretext to wander all about London in search of concretizes her writings; around this slight object, time wraps itself, cylindrical or circular. Thought becomes act as she walks, her stride measured by the search for a pencil, as if her wandering were to be sketched out by the pencil lead, until she returns home.

A further object lesson is given by the distressing story about the reflection of an empty life: "The Lady in the Looking Glass." She is the American painter Ethel Sands, one of the significant persons acting as intermediary between the Bloomsbury group and France, living with her partner, the painter Nan Hudson, near Dieppe. Many of the group spent time in their house, called Auppegard, in the little village of Offranville, by the ferry route between England and France: Roger Fry, Duncan Grant, Vanessa Bell, Lytton Strachey, Virginia Woolf. The pitiless observation by the author of these ladies so taken with things and their neat ordering—muslin, she writes, placed even over fly excrement—reveals an empty vessel of a life.

Here is a passage from the tale that I find telling:

> There were her grey-green dress, and her long shoes, her basket, and something sparkling at her throat. . . . At once the looking-glass began to pour over her a light that seemed to fix her; that seemed like some acid to bite off the unessential and superficial and to leave only the truth. . . . Everything dropped from her—clouds, dress, basket, diamond– all that one had called the creeper and convolvulus. Here was the hard wall beneath. Here was the woman herself. . . . And there was nothing. (*Shorter Fiction* 224–25)

Of the two translations of "The Lady in the Looking-Glass" ("La Dame au miroir"), Pierre Nordon's, in a bilingual edition, presents Woolf as a difficult modernist writer to the uninitiated student:

> Ils étaient là, sa robe gris-vert, ses longs souliers, son panier et l'objet qui étincelait à son cou. . . . Tout la quitta: nuages, robe, panier, brillant, tout ce qui avait fait office de lierre et de volubilis. La dure muraille était dévoilée. La véritable femme dévoilée. . . . Et il n'y avait rien. Isabella était totalement vide. ("La Dame," trans. Nordon, 177)

And then there is a superb rendering by Hélène Bokanowski:

> Sa robe gris-vert, ses longs souliers, son panier et quelque chose
> qui brillait à son cou, tout était là. . . . Tout la quitta—les nuages,
> la robe, le panier, le diamant—tout ce que l'on avait intitulé plante
> grimpante et volubilis. Seul demeurait le mur solide. La véritable
> femme demeurait seule. . . . Et il n'y avait rien. ("La Dame," trans.
> Bokanowski, 203)

To enumerate the objects first—dress, delicate shoes, and basket—
before summing it up: "tout était là" ("everything was there" or
"that's all there was") is a stroke of genius, as opposed to stating
first that one is going to enumerate them: "ils étaient là" ("they were
there"). For the point is precisely that *the appearance precedes the
essence*, and that the latter is what turns out to be lacking. That the
too hard "objet" should not be called upon to translate the deliberately unfocused "something" seems apparent to me, for exactly
that imprecise "something" is what gives room to the mind and the
imagination. "Quelque chose" grasps the something, while leaving
it fluid. In the second translation, the specificity of the article: "les
nuages, la robe, le panier, le diamant" ("the clouds, the dress, the
basket, the diamond") followed by the intrusion of the other: "tout
ce que l'on avait intitulé" ("everything that had been called") make
the stripping of the lady's attributes more brutal, more real, more
terrible.

Take another object: the presentation of the pool itself, in "The
Fascination of the Pool," instantly displays its depth, its secret at-
traction, and the fact that it elides any elucidation, as well as its reflective nature on which its brief being closes. This fascination is
precisely the one sensed by the reader of Virginia Woolf in her major texts: depth, reflective power, elision. Its opening, already constructed about an elision, is so full of verbal recalls as to test the skill
of the translator who must not fall into heavy-handedness. The story,
based on impenetrability and on reflection, turns about a sign at its
center and placed also in the center of the pool. So it is about semi-
otics and about secrets, and has to be translated with subtlety.

Here is the opening of the original, with a masterly translation by
Josée Kamoun following it:

It may have been very deep—certainly one could not see to the bottom of it. Round the edge was so thick a fringe of rushes that their reflections made a darkness like the darkness of very deep water. (*Shorter Fiction* 226)

ैa

Il était peut-être très profond—insondable à l'oeil en tout cas. Ses bords étaient frangés de joncs si touffus que leur reflet était ombreux comme l'ombre des eaux profondes. ("La Fascination" 157)

The translation manages to keep the reflection from deep to deep: "profond . . . profondes"), and the echo from dark to dark ("ombreux . . . ombre"), and to omit precisely what is invisible to the eye. It replaces the "bottom of it" that "one could not see" by the simple word that says it cannot be plumbed or sounded: "insondable" does not say one cannot see, but that it cannot be even measured. A perfect solution.

As for elision, Woolf's translators practice it frequently—shades of Mallarmé's elision of a stanza in Tennyson. . . . Even Viviane Forrester's superb rendering of *Three Guineas* omits an essential passage of the Woolf original. The translated text moves from "le velours, la soie, la fourrure et l'hermine" ("the velvet, the silk, the fur and the ermine") directly to "Hélas! Cette prospection, ce survol de la situation sont loin d'être encourageants" ("Alas! This bird's-eye view of the situation, this overlooking, are far from encouraging") (*Trois Guinées* 63), thus eliminating four essential sentences about educated men emphasizing "their superiority over other people," emotions that encourage a "disposition towards war . . ." (*Three Guineas*, 21).

Take another example of a highly peculiar moment in a translation of Virginia Woolf into French by Clara Malraux. The famous removal of the Khmer statues from Cambodia by André and Clara was of a different order from the removal of part of Woolf's sentence from a French translation, but somewhat analogous to it. For this suppression of a crucial part illustrates in a metapoetic fashion the dangers involved in overlooking any part of a Woolf text, since its heart may be located somewhere the rational mind may not know to look: right in the middle of some sentence, after some harmless comma, hedged in and about by elements less crucial. The moral of the story may be right there, where we least expect it, which is part of my story, concerning the crucial object of translating such a subtle and complicated author.

Here is the famous passage toward the end of *A Room of One's Own* concerning Shakespeare's sister:

> For my belief is that . . . if we look past Milton's bogey, for no human being should shut out the view; if we face the fact, for it is a fact, that there is no arm to cling to, but that we go alone and that our relation is to the world of reality and not only to the world of men and women, and then the opportunity will come and the dead poet who was Shakespeare's sister will put on the body which she has so often laid down. (118)

Now the translation of this by Clara Malraux reads well, with one glaring exception:

> Car voici ma conviction . . . si nous parvenons à regarder plus loin que le croque-mitaine de Milton—car aucun être humain, si nous ne reculons pas devant le fait (car c'est bien là un fait) qu'il n'y a aucun bras auquel nous accrocher et que nous marchons seules et que nous sommes en relation avec le monde de la réalité et non seulement avec le monde des hommes et des femmes—alors l'occasion se présentera pour la poétesse morte qui était la soeur de Shakespeare de prendre cette forme humaine à là qu'elle il lui a si souvent fallu renoncer. (*Une Chambre* 170–71)

Strangely, what is omitted here is precisely that shutting out of the view, which is surely the point. Its disappearance is like some gigantic pointer signaling exactly what could be overlooked in a Poe-like reading. The too-big object simply disappears in the hedges.

In circular fashion, I return to "The Mark on the Wall," where interruptions, delay, and return so matter. I want to pick up now one detail of the English:

> I must jump up and see for myself what that mark on the wall really is—a nail, a rose-leaf, a crack in the wood?

And it continues:

Wood is a pleasant thing to think about. It comes from a tree; and trees grow, and we don't know how they grow. (*Shorter Fiction* 88)

It is clear right here, in this moment, that delight is associated with thought, and with the lack of knowledge. We think about, we delight in thinking about, that which we do not yet know, like this wood and this tree. Thought radiates out from the center, not in a straight line: this is modernism, the nonlinear. See what grows and permits growth, and what does not.

It is the contemporary poet Francis Ponge who made the most explicit of object lessons for us. In his many investigations of separate things—a cigarette, an oyster, a blackberry, a stone—he has shown what can be spun out of the thing. His essay on the pebble, found in the 1945 issue of *View*, relates to Woolf's perspective on objects. In his "New Introduction to the Pebble," Ponge maintains that by looking into whatever object we focus on closely enough, we will ourselves become part of it:

> The real secret of the contemplator's success is in his refusal to consider as *an evil* the encroachment on his personality by things. . . .
>
> I suggest for each the opening of inside trapdoors, a voyage into the depth of things, an invasion of qualities, a revolution or subversion comparable to the kind that the plough or shovel effects when, all at once and for the first time, millions of particles, flakes, roots, worms and little creatures previously buried are brought to light. O infinite resources in the depth of things, *produced by* the infinite resources of the semantic depth of words! (45)

A *delay in wood* like Marcel Duchamp's *Delay in Glass*. So, as that undefined mark on the wall, in its very undefinition, permits the observing imagination to wander, as that pencil with its profile so slight permits an entire voyage around London, as that lump of glass, so unrecognizable to any but the man possessed by it, allows his entire mental being to be, these objects will prevent our ever falling into the vacancy of a mirror. For, around the thing chosen, the person perceiving and living grows, like a tree without our knowing how. Like so many rings marking age and celebrating growth itself, the kind that moves in circles, not in lines. The modernist kind.

Comparing Charles Mauron's superb translation of *Orlando* with another, competent but undistinguished, is to see how fully justified is Virginia Woolf's faith in Mauron as a translator. Mauron—Roger Fry's good friend and the translator of Mallarmé, E. M. Forster, T. E. Lawrence, and D. H. Lawrence—also translated Woolf's *Flush* and the middle section of *To the Lighthouse*, but I will limit myself to the case of *Orlando* and to a very few passages within it.

In the case of Woolf, as in others, it is often the colorfulness of English that the formalities of French so often fail to grasp, sometimes through the fault of the language, but sometimes again through a certain lack of imagination that makes its irremediable mark upon the translated text. It falls flat, untouched by Woolf's quirky genius. Mauron's translation conveys just the bends and stretches and funniness of the original.

Compare these texts:

> For once the disease of reading has laid hold upon the system it weakens it so that it falls an easy prey to that other scourge which dwells in the ink pot and festers in the quill. The wretch takes to writing . . . a poor man, whose only property is a chair and table set beneath a leaky roof. . . . (*Orlando* 48)
>
> ૱
>
> Une fois que la maladie de la lecture exerce son emprise sur l'organisme, elle l'affaiblit tant que l'individu devient une proie facile pour cet autre fléau qui gite dans l'encrier et couve sous la plume. Le malheureux se met à écrire . . . une chaise et une table sous un toit qui prend de l'eau. (*Orlando*, trans. Pappo-Musard, 56)
>
> ૱
>
> Quand cette peste de lecture s'est emparée de l'homme, elle l'affaiblit tant qu'il devient une proie facile pour l'autre fléau—celui qui se tapit au fond de l'encrier et purule au bout de la plume. Le malheureux est pris de la rage d'écrire . . . sa chaise et sa table branlantes sous un toit crevassé. (*Orlando*, trans. Mauron, 605)

The roof is indeed leaking, it takes in water, but the cause is, of course, that the roof is "crevassé," a word that you can roll around in your mouth. You can feel the Provençal joy in words in Mauron's translations, rich with the humor and high color of French, working to their full extent a conscious and consciously understood exaggeration. So the writing wretch is not just taken with a "maladie" but with "la peste," and this plague does not just hatch in the quill—"couve"—but actually festers there: "purule." This wretch does not just start to write, as in the other translation ("se met à écrire") but is actually seized by madness: "pris de la rage," and so on.

What else he captures—here and elsewhere, and quite astonishingly—is the rhythm of the English. When Woolf breaks off, over and over, in a tease, he does precisely the same thing, never missing a beat. Instead of Pappo-Musard's quite correct "Une chaise et une table sous un toit qui prend l'eau," he brings the scene into close-up, with rapidity: the poor man's chair, his table, his broken roof . . . of course, a roof in need of repair lets water in, no need to say it!

And yet at times, when the humor is quieter in the original, he can be quieter.

> Here she took up her lodging and began instantly to look about her for what she had come in search of—that is to say, life and a lover. (190)

The wit here, of course, resides in the irony of the confidence of our hero/ine in the notion of the instant availability of those things, and others. Mauron speeds on even more quickly: putting a simple colon after what she had come in search of . . . "That is to say," which does the trick neatly:

> Aussitôt installée, Orlando se mit en quête. Elle était venue chercher à la ville: la vie et un amant. (123)

The other translation is quite correct but does not wear its irony so crucially upon its sleeve:

> C'est donc là quelle s'établit et qu'elle se mit immédiatement en quête de ce qu'elle était venue chercher: c'est-à-dire, la vie et un amant. (*Orlando*, trans. Pappo-Musard, 674)

Another passage in *Orlando* seems to be modeled on the formal model of the celebrated *Comices* scene in Flaubert's *Madame Bovary*, in which the interruption outside and the seduction inside are set in an implicit/explicit dialogue for the amusement of the reader. Woolf, too, plays here on the in and out of it all:

> Is nothing, then, going to happen this pale March morning to mitigate, to veil, to cover, to conceal, to shroud this undeniable event whatever it may be? For after giving that sudden, violent start, Orlando—but Heaven be praised, at this very moment there struck up outside one of these frail, reedy, fluty, jerky, old-fashioned barrel-organs which are still sometimes played by Italian organ-grinders in back streets. Let us accept the intervention, humble though it is, as if it were the music of the spheres, and allow it, with all its gasps and groans, to fill this page with sound . . . let the barrel-organ sound and transport us on thought, which is no more than a little boat, when music sounds, tossing on the waves; on thought, which is, of all carriers, the most clumsy, the most erratic, over the roof tops and the back gardens. . . . (292–93)
>
> ❧
>
> Ne va-t-il donc rien arriver, en cette pâle matinée de mars, pour atténuer, voiler, recouvrir, envelopper cet événement (quelqu'il soit), indéniable? Car, après avoir sursauté de façon si soudaine et si violente, Orlando . . . Mais Dieu soit loué, juste à cet instant monta du dehors, frêle, sifflotant, fluté, sautillant , démodé, le chant d'un orgue de Barbarie. . . . Acceptons cette intervention, si humble que nous la jugions, comme si elle était la musique des sphères, et permettons-lui, avec ses hoquets et ses grognements, de remplir du moins cette page. . . . (*Orlando*, trans. Mauron, 182)

Here the wit about the event (whatever it is) is undeniable. And it is the wit that counts, as well as the deliberate delay of the sound of the organ, and the rough-and-tumble nature of the "hoquets et ses grognements." The subtle irony of its being allowed, if not to fill the universe, to fill at least this page, is undeniably rendered.

> Rien ne va-t-il donc arriver, en cette pâle matinée de mars, pour atténuer, voiler, couvrir, dissimuler, déguiser cet événement indénia-ble, quelle que soit la nature! Car après avoir soudain et violem-ment sursauté, Orlando. . . . Mais, le ciel soit loué, au même in-

stant résonna dehors l'un de ces vieux orgues de Barbarie, fragiles, nasillard, flutés, saccadés, dont jouent encore. . . . Acceptons cette intervention, aussi humble soit-elle, comme si c'était la musique des sphères, et permettons à l'instrument, qui halète et ahane, de remplir de bruit cette page. . . . (*Orlando*, trans. Pappo-Musard, 735)

For me the final clincher is a combination of two brief and impossible-to-render play on words, the second repeating and teasing about the first, both of which have their play in rhyme—so that the translation, too, has to play on rhyme or all is lost. Here, Mauron makes the very best of a difficult situation, and that is surely one of the best ways to judge any translation:

. . . and to be taking from its case a cigarette or cigar even, and to be flinging a cloak under (as the rhyme requires) an oak. . . . And we rise, and our eyes (for how handy a rhyme is to pass us safe over the awkward transition from death to life) fall on—(here the barrel-organ stops playing abruptly). (293–95)

. . . et qu'on prend dans son étui une cigarette, ou même un cigare, et qu'on étale son manteau sous (la rime l'exige) un ormeau. . . . Alors nous nous redressons et nos yeux abaissons (car une rime s'avère bien utile pour franchir sain et sauf le col malaisé qui sépare la mort de la vie) sur. . . . (Mais l'orgue de Barbarie s'interrompt soudain.) (*Orlando*, trans. Pappo-Musard, 736–37)

. . . et encore prendre dans son étui une cigarette ou même un cigare, jeter son manteau (comme la rime le demande) sous un ormeau. . . . Et nous nous levons, et nos regards vont (comme une chanson est commode pour nous aider à franchir sans encombre la pénible transition de la mort à la vie!) tomber—(l'orgue de Barbarie s'arrête net). (*Orlando*, trans. Mauron, 182–84)

This is not a simple repetition of the rhyme: repetition of sound, but a deliberately awkward rendering in order to make fun of it all. That, after all, is often the point. Mauron knows how to have fun and how to share it. This is, I submit, one of the goals of such a translation.

The Waves is surely the most difficult of Woolf's writing to render
in another language, given its lyricism and subtle shifts of voice.
The two major translations so far of this work are by the famous
writer and academician Marguerite Yourcenar and by Cécile Wajsbrot; they are radically different. Each has its champions; I have my
own opinion, as will be clear.

In Margaret Yourcenar's translation of *The Waves*, her classicizing
view is clear. She sees it as one of those light and lovely "tapestries
full of flowers and birds, never exposing indiscreetly in the work the
fatigue, and the secret of the often painful sap in which the lovely
wool has been dipped" (*Vagues*, trans. Yourcenar, 212). In spite of
her own brilliance of writing, her rendering of Virginia Woolf, unlike the more recent one by Cécile Wajsbrot, is literal-minded, veering toward the novelistic and the narrative as opposed to the poetic and deliberately "subjectless" and rhythmical text that Woolf
wanted for her poem-novel. Wajsbrot points out that Woolf plunged
down into feeling, whereas Yourcenar remains on the surface: "Le
regard de Virginia Woolf plonge, celui de Marguerite Yourcenar par-
court" ("Virginia Woolf's gaze dives down; Marguerite Yourcenar's
skims along") (*Vagues*, trans. Wajsbrot, 31). True enough, but while
Yourcenar's gaze may skim, her language is heavy.

Never does Yourcenar omit a pointing word, a situating adverb,
those elements that can stop a lyric flow as straight in its tracks as
we are stopped by her view of Lily Briscoe in *To the Lighthouse*:
"la pauvre Miss Briscoe, dont la terne existence s'est usée à peindre
d'assez médiocres toiles qu'elle ne parvient jamais à finir" ("poor
Miss Briscoe, whose dull existence has worn itself out in painting rather mediocre canvases she never manages to finish") (trans.
Yourcenar, 211). How could someone viewing Lily Briscoe in this
literalizing fashion translate *The Waves* otherwise?

For a passage describing Susan's gait and Bernard's and Susan's
view of things, the two translations give an entirely different feeling. Here is the original: "Now she walks across the field with a
swing, nonchalantly. . . . There is agitation and trouble here. There
is gloom. . . ." And then Bernard's voice: "Now we have fallen
through the tree-tops to the earth." And Susan: "I see the lady writ-

ing. I see the gardeners sweeping" (*Waves* 11–14). Yourcenar's version: "Voici qu'elle traverse le champ avec un balancement nonchalant. . . . Tout ici est plein de trouble et d'agitation. Tout est lugubre." And for Bernard: "Et maintenant, nous voilà tombés à travers les hautes branches des arbres, sur la terre. . . ." Susan continues, appearing as heavy as before: "Je vois la dame qui écrit. Je vois les jardiniers qui balayent . . ." (219–21). Instead of these leaden phrases, Wajsbrot gives the far lighter: "Maintenant, elle traverse le champ d'un air dégagé. . . . Il y a de l'agitation et du chagrin. Une mélancolie" (40). And Bernard: "Maintenant, nous sommes tombés des arbres." Then Susan again, freer in tone than in Yourcenar's version: "Je vois la dame écrire. Je vois les jardiniers balayer" (43).

Or take Jinny's utterly simple statement of hereness and nowness, and imminent action: " 'This is here,' said Jinny, 'this is now. But soon we shall go' " (19). For which Yourcenar gives the very long: " 'Ce que vous dites, c'est vrai ici où nous sommes,' dit Jinny, 'c'est vrai en ce moment. Mais il faudra bientôt nous en aller' " (224–25). In Wajsbrot's version, the perception retains, in its brevity, the immediacy and simplicity of the original: " 'Nous sommes ici,' dit Jinny, 'et maintenant. Mais nous allons partir' " (47). The difference is in the rhythm. The earlier and heavier version slows down Woolf's delicate and rapid immediacy of perception, that sense of the moment, to a plodding gait, almost a standstill.

Yourcenar spells things out as Virginia Woolf does not. Here is the end of Bernard's original meal:

> Now the meal is finished; we are surrounded by peelings and bread-crumbs. I have tried to break off this bunch and hand it you; but whether there is substance or truth in it I do not know. Nor do I know exactly where we are. (288)

For which Yourcenar gives:

> Et maintenant, le repas est terminé; nous sommes entourés de pelures de fruits et de miettes de pain. J'ai essayé de cueillir cette grappe (ma vie?) et de vous l'offrir: mais je ne sais pas moi-même ce qu'elle contient de réalité. Et je ne sais même pas exactement où nous sommes. (413)

Compare Wajsbrot's translation, knowing there is no need to spell out the fruit under the peeling, taking the minor risk of crumbs without bread, finding virtue in the literal gesture of holding out the fruit, as in the original: "hand it you" and not simply the more general "offer it you." Her translation believes, as does the original, in the continuity of knowledge and its lack, not the ordinary joining of "et" ("Et je ne sais même pas") and knows it to be conceptually crucial, in the negative comparative of "no more than"—"pas plus que":

> Maintenant, le repas est fini; nous sommes entourés de miettes et d'épluchures. J'ai essayé de détacher la grappe, de vous la tendre; contient-elle une substance, une vérité, je ne sais pas. Pas plus que je ne sais exactement où nous sommes. (242)

Why does it matter? Because literalism commits the major sin against writing that flows, thought that is complex, and rhythm that is crafted—it flattens them all. To compare the plodding translations of Yourcenar with those of Mauron and Wajsbrot is not just to see what a literalizing gait does to poetry, but, more positively, to see why Roger Fry was indebted to and impassioned about Charles Mauron's mind and his ability to communicate the work of another's mind. The translation of mental complexity is a difficult, crucial, feather-delicate thing.

VI. *Pound at Liberty*

HUGH KENNER'S INTRODUCTION to the New Directions volume of Pound's translations lauds the boldness with which the new form Pound finds "permanently extends the bounds of English verse" (Pound 9). The translator's task, claims Kenner, "must be a kind of seeing" (10). And once his grasp of the original emotion is firm and contextualized, neither it nor the version he arrives at is likely to wobble. (We recognize the "wobble" from Pound's own vocabulary.) Sometimes, says Kenner, Pound makes a "slightly wrong meaning" into a "completely right feeling" (12).

As a poet, Pound repoetizes and—or so it seems to me—generally in the manner the poets he translates would have enjoyed their poems. Making them briefer, jumping to conclusions, slangifying them.

> Say what you will in two
> Words and get thru.
> Long, frilly
> Palaver is silly
> (Air: "Sentir Avec Ardeur"; Pound's translation from the Marquise de Boufflers [1711–1786], 433)

I will be considering only the French and the Provençal poems he translated, making them into Pound-like texts: this is particularly sensible in the cases of Arnaut Daniel, Charles d'Orléans, Joachim du Bellay, Jules Laforgue, and Arthur Rimbaud, with whom I am chiefly concerned. The entire Rimbaldian myth of revolution combines with the difficult-to-swallow side of the slave trader, both of them corresponding to the complications of Pound: his revolutionary poetics and then his fascist side. What rescues both of them is their uncompromising disregard for the social niceties accepted by so many.

In Pound's translations of the troubadours, quite often the feeling comes from the last line of each stanza or strophe having the same concluding rhyme and rhythm. Two poems from Arnaut Daniel will illustrate this, the first taken from the "Chanson do'ill mot" ("Chansson Doil"), which affirms immediately how the poet will work with nature, and where each stanza takes this classic and seemly form:

> I'll make a song   with exquisite
> Clear words, for buds are blowing sweet
> Where the sprays meet,
> And flowers don
> Their bold blazon
> Where leafage springeth greenly
> O'ershadowing
> The birds that sing
> And cry in coppice seemly.
> (Pound 145)

Pound had certainly read Gerard Manley Hopkins and those very grand and desolate poems called "the terrible sonnets," one of them beginning:

> My own heart let me more have pity on; let
> Me live to my sad self hereafter kind
> (Hopkins 63)

It ends with the enjambment stretched to an apostrophe and the notion of in-betweenness, creating a verb: to "betweenpie," so that the pied beauty of the sky can stretch between the mountains as that previous verb "smile's" stretches between the verses:

. . . let joy size
At God knows when to God knows what; whose smile
's not wrung, see you; unforeseen times rather—as skies
Betweenpie mountains—lights a lovely mile.

(Hopkins 63)

The fifth stanza of this same Poundian translation of Daniel goes like this, after the Provençal:

Though my swath long   's run wavering,
My thoughts go forth to thee and cling,
Wherefore I sing
Of joys replete
Once, where our feet
Parted, and mine eyes plainly
Show mists begun
And sweetly undone,
For joy's the pain doth burn me.
(145)

The poem concludes:

Save 'neath Love's thong I move no thing,
And my way brooks no measuring,
For right hath spring
In that Love's heat
Was ne'er complete
As mine, since Adam.   'Tween me
And sly treason
No net is spun,
Wherefore my joy grows greenly.

CODA

Lady, whoe'er demean thee
My benison
Is set upon
Thy grace where it moves queenly.
(145)

But it gets even better. Take the beginning of a few stanzas or strophes of the same poet:

> Tot quant es gela,
> Mas ieu non puesc frezir,
> C'amors novela
> Mi fal cor reverdir;
> (144)

Which I roughly translate as:

> Quand tout ici est de glace,
> Néanmoins je ne puis geler,
> Car un nouvel amour
> Fait reverdir mon coeur . . .

And in English:

> Though all things freeze here,
> I can naught feel the cold,
> For my new love sees, here
> my heart's new leaf unfold . . .
> (144)

And a few lines later:

> Bona es vida,
> Pos joia la mante . . .

My rough translation:

> Bonne est la vie
> Puisque la joie la maintient.

And in English:

> Aye, life's a high thing,
> where joy's his maintenance . . .
> (144)

One more beginning:

> Bona doctrina e soaus
> E cors clars, sotils e francs
> M'an d'Amor al ferm conduich

My rough translation:

> La bonne et suave pensée
> Et le coeur clair, subtil et franc,
> M'ont conduit jusqu'au fort de l'Amour
> ❧
> The gracious thinking and the frank
> Clear and quick perceiving heart
> Have led me to the fort of love
> (169)

Sometimes accidents lead to discoveries. Taking a bus up Madison Avenue that collided with another bus in front of it, I was obliged to step off and take another. So doing, I met a fellow translator and memoirist, who translates from Occitan, like Pound, and who regaled me with the following story of a mistake, which she has written about. I transcribe her story of the story:

Arnaut Daniel Speaks His Reasons
POSTSCRIPT
We souls see into the future. Six centuries from now, my songs will be revealed to the New World by an ambitious young poet writing in the lingo of *yes*. He will attempt to renew that tongue. By giving his fellow poets lessons in *oc* and *si*, he will teach "The Spirit of Romance." He will misread my signature line

> *Ieu soi Arnaut che amas l'aura*

and write: "I am Arnaut who *loves* the air." Absurd. If I'd loved plentiful, sweet air, I wouldn't have chased the hare with a bull or swum against the current (he got those lines right). It was the struggle to "*gather* (*amasar*) the air" and to grasp other unattainable objects that prompted all my poems. (White, unpublished ms.)

Now, what a wonderful mistake! "Gathers" is grand, and, from my point of view, "love" is no less so. Sorry about the mistake, Arnaut, but I like to think that love is one of the best that one can make. . . .

As for Pound's translations of Arthur Rimbaud, brilliant in every way, I will start with one of his suppressions. In the fearful poem called "Venus anadyomène," Pound simply eliminates the last two stanzas, with the gory detail of the ulcer in the anus, and ends like this:

> Puis les rondeurs des reins semblent prendre l'essor;
> La graisse sous la peau paraît en feuilles plates.
> (Rimbaud 61)
>
> ₰
>
> And the fat, in clumsy slabs beneath the skin,
> Seems ready to emerge without further aids.
> (Pound 416)

And that is because *enough is enough*. He softens the poem without undoing the clumsiness, eliminates the more uncomfortable last two stanzas, and suppresses the CLARA VENUS, who will not be sorely missed. For those who cling to exactitude, this ain't exact. No more than Tennyson's "Mariana" received an exact translation, second time around, from Mallarmé. But, from my point of view, it is a fine choice. And in Pound the poet, there remains always a certain discretion, humanizing the young cruelty of Rimbaud.

Rimbaud's "Première soirée," translated by Pound as "Comedy in Three Caresses," is an informal delight:

> Elle était fort déshabillée
> Et de grands arbres indiscrets
> Aux vitres jetaient leur feuillée
> Malinement, tout près, tout près.
> (Rimbaud 62–63)
>
> ₰
>
> She hadn't much left on, and the big trees,
> With no discretion, swished
> Their leaves over the window-pane
> Teasingly, so near, so near.
> (Pound 434–35)

It is, as often, the details that count here, such as the addition of the "left" instead of "she hadn't much on." As the *dés-* can mean the result of an action or not, the "left" adds the action, while the indiscretion of the trees in their sweep set the scene for another and more human indiscretion, teasingly. The easiness of the little feet, the little quiver, the smallness of the seduction—it doesn't take much, just right, as she says: "Ooooh, that's better"—give a small tweak to the tease:

Sur le plancher frissonnaient d'aise
Ses petits pieds si fins, si fins
 ʒₐ
And her little toes tickled the floor
Quivering comfortably, and so small.

Of course the doubling of the detail as in "little" and "small" fits the tickle perfectly, in the general comfiness of the tone, and picks up on the "so near, so near" . . . "si fins, si fins," which equals "and so small." The "and so small" compensates for the "si, si" or "so, so." Pound exercises a delicate craft.

In the original, "un petit rayon buissonnier"—*buisson*, "bush"—gives sprouting, by extension, while the "papillonner dans son sourire," like a smile, extends the metaphor itself, spreading it gently over the breast. To render "ses fines chevilles" by "her traced ankles" marks the delicacy of the outline, leaping the middle term "fines" to arrive at the same feeling as a result:

Elle eut un doux rire brutal
 ʒₐ
And she smiled a longish smile, bad sign

To render "doux" ("sweet") as "longish" is the perfect opposition for the "brutal"—and to render the latter as "bad" is Pound-like witty.

"Scampered under her shift"—this renders "les petits pieds sous la chemise / se sauvèrent" quite as if the hiding under were a fleeing away, which in a sense it is.

Le rire feignait de punir!

꙳

The smile pretending coldness?

This punctuational shift from the exclamation point (!) to the question mark (?) puts in coy doubt the pretended cold—that she was only feigning ("feignait"):

> Elle jeta sa tête mièvre
> En arrière: "Oh! C'est encor mieux!"
>
> ꙳
>
> And she threw back her weakling head:
> "That's better now," she said.
>
> ꙳
>
> —Je lui jetai le reste au sein
>
> ꙳
>
> I chucked the rest between her breasts . . .

Sure. Why indeed not make light of her speech, and of the whole light occasion?

> Dans un baiser, qui la fit rire
> D'un bon rire qui voulait bien . . .
>
> ꙳
>
> In a caress that brought a kindly smile
> Benevolence, all of it.

And here, of course, instead of suggestion and incompletion, we are given an absolute assurance and completion. For one last change, in the original, there is one exact repetition:

> Elle était fort déshabillée
> Et de grands arbres indiscrets
> Aux vitres jetaient leur feuillée
> Malinement, tout près, tout près.
> (Rimbaud 62–63)

Whereas the English reduces four lines to three, to speed it up, and ends:

> She hadn't much left on, and the big trees
> Swished their leaves over the window-pane
> At ease, teasingly, and so near.
> (Pound 434–35)

The ease that her little toes showed before is now incorporated in the text right where it happens, next to the "teasingly," which has eased itself. The formerly indiscreet branches have now given leave to a leaf, itself leading, inevitably and perfectly, to the past tense of "leave": "not much left on."

Pound takes the suggestion and makes it a realization, takes the indecision and makes it a decision. Three caresses: kiss her ankles, kiss her eyelids, chuck her "something still" between her breasts, making of it a "comedy in three acts," just as the title had it.

The feeling seems to be kept at every level—clearly, this is an anti-mimetic procedure, and just as clearly, the result sounds like Pound as much as Rimbaud. In such translations (unlike those of Mallarmé, say), the translator is as recognizable as the poet—it turns out to be a double work.

In Pound's version of Rimbaud's "Les Chercheuses de poux" as the "Lice-Hunters," we again recognize the touch: informal, witty, breezy. For straight off, the original "enfant" becomes a "kid," such informality totally in accord with the detail of the lice and their hunters, these magic-fingered goddesses with their slow sensuality, their slender fingers and silvery nails, who come to his bedroom:

> Et dans ses lourds cheveux où tombe la rosée
> Promènent leurs doigts fins, terribles et charmeurs.
>
> ❧
>
> And run fine, alluring, terrible
> Fingers through his thick dew-matted hair.

Below, the sibilants ("sifflement," "salives") reinforce the sensuality to the point of saturation, and then, suddenly, the interruption works like the sensuality of a stutter:

> Et qu'interrompt parfois un sifflement, salives
> Reprises sur la lèvre ou désirs de baisers.

Or broken anon, sibilant, the saliva's hiss
Drawn from a lip, or a desire to kiss.

Like the "kid," the "neath" reinforces the willed informality of the scene:

L'enfant se sent, selon la lenteur des caresses
Sourdre et mourir sans cesse un désir de pleurer.
꒳
. . . And the kid feels
Neath the slowness of their caresses, constantly
Wane and fade a desire to cry.

No, his desire has become something else already, quite like that desire to kiss.

Voilà que monte en lui le vin de la Paresse
꒳
And Lo! there mounts within him Wine of Laziness
(Rimbaud 127; Pound 436)

Something in Pound loves to exacerbate the slowness, always like some rhythmic tease, recalling that "Comedy in Three Caresses."

One of Pound's triumphs of brevity is the splendidly bright and colored "Au Cabaret-Vert, cinq heures du soir," in which the combination of joyousness and rapidity makes of this nineteenth-century poem a present-day paean to easygoingness.

Here, Pound starts with what matters: that is, the wearing out of the young man's shoes, after a week of walking, compensated by the deliciousness of the repast, simple and vivid:

—*Au Cabaret-Vert:* je demandai des tartines
De beurre et du jambon qui fût à moitié froid.
Bienheureux, j'allongeai les jambes sous la table
Verte . . .
(Rimbaud 77)
꒳

Bread, butter, at the Green Cabaret
And the ham half cold.

So, in the Green Cabaret, there is a great comfort:

Got my legs stretched out . . .
(Pound 434)

Now here there is clearly no need for any table, green or otherwise, and Pound always suppresses whatever details he can, for greater vitality. To that vitality, the utter informality adds "la fille aux tétons énormes" with her nice plumpness, which becomes a

Gal with the big bubs

And at the same temperature and of the same pleasing plumpness, the lukewarm ham and a great mug of foaming beer make, in the gilding sunlight, part of the perfect still life with its pink flesh, its white fat, and its metonymic sprig of garlic, precisely not a whole head or a sharp-sounding clove. Even the sprig is sprouting. . . .

In Pound's renderings of or homages to Rimbaud, there is a constant sort of happiness sensible in all the details and in the whole. Pound's great sureness of himself as poet permits him to take many liberties, making the entire repertoire of Rimbaud/Pound an informal, joyous, hearty, but non-vulgar Pound we might not have suspected.

I want now to return to Arnaut Daniel once more, from his song "Of High All-Attaining." Whatever application we would turn it toward in our individual lives—translating, loving, and living—we could do worse than to dwell for a time at least in the light Pound has it shed:

Nor think my heart will ever be less fain,
The flame is in my head and burns unwaning.
(419)

VII. *Beckett's Business*

A WRITER WHO has no thoughts about his own work, or says he does not—this partisan of a "literature of the unword" (Beckett, *Disjecta* 12) that Beckett declares himself to be—how should he be so given to the art of translation? Surely that art is about words as it is about work. Beckett's ironies themselves need translating. In any case, his often peculiar perspective has a multiplying, generative effect on our own.

In both his books on Beckett, Hugh Kenner signals some translation problems. In his *Samuel Beckett*, he emphasizes the difficulty of Beckett's translation of the dialogue in *Endgame* from the original French: "he has had to prune the English very considerably to keep sentiment out" (95). For example, the English version of an extensive passage in French in *Fin de partie* omits a good part, or is, as Kenner puts it, "inexplicably sketchy" (*Reader's Guide* 58). Yet another suppression in translation . . . The omitted version concerns the figure of a boy first taken for a leaf, a flower, a tomato, in rapid succession, before arriving at the expression of a nostalgia projected by the narrator on to the boy, gazing at his navel: "Il regarde la maison sans doute, avec les yeux de Moïse mourant" (*Reader's Guide* 94). Just so, the reading of Beckett calls upon all the available layers of memory of other texts and authors that we might have at our disposal. Not that we always know what exactly he has read—but

Beckettian thought calls upon all our resources and opens the way for their deployment.

In this example, those readers haunted by the ghost of French literature may well hear in this expression another nostalgia. For the phrase "Il regarde la maison sans doute, avec les yeux de Moïse mourant" ("He looks at the house, doubtless, with the eyes of the dying Moses"), for all its irony in the "doubtless," might seem to conflate a memory of Alfred de Vigny's poems "La Maison du berger," "La Mort du loup," and his great "Moïse" ("The Shepherd's House," "The Death of the Wolf," and "Moses"). It at least permits our backward reflection on this triple potential source. And so, in the bilingual presentation of Beckett's *Collected Poems in English and French*, our reading of his French haunts, as is natural, our reading of his English translations. The latter undergo a certain development between the years from 1932 to 1975, from Beckett's versions of Paul Éluard's surrealist poems, faithful or "close" as they are, to the immensely witty and concise versions of eight of Sébastien Chamfort's *maximes*, entitled "Long After Chamfort."

Let me start, then, by the end of this volume. The most recent translations within it are quite simply hilarious. The maxims of Sébastien-Roch Nicolas de Chamfort were originally uttered as quips in various salons; after his suicide in 1794, in the reign of the Terror, they were gathered with his thoughts and anecdotes in a posthumous publication (Beckett, *Collected Poems* 122–37). Beckett's more than witty condensations of them are so concentrated as to be reminiscent of his spoof of a manifesto of "Le concentrisme," or "Concentrism," invented by one Jean du Chas (*Disjecta* 35–42). These joyous translations are done in a spirit of absolute confidence of mind:

> Quand on soutient que les gens les moins sensibles sont à tout prendre, les plus heureux, je me rappelle le proverbe indien: "Il vaut mieux être assis que debout, couché que assis, mort que tout cela."

> Better on your arse than on your feet,
> Flat on your back than either, dead than the lot.
> (*Collected Poems* 126–27)

One of Beckett's early translations from his English to his French, with a nine-year span between the two—the English written in 1937 and the French in 1946—shows irony and tragedy mixed.

English version, 1937

they come
different and the same
with each it is different and the same
with each the absence of love is different
with each the absence of love is the same

&

French translation, 1946

elles viennent
autres et pareilles
avec chacune c'est autre et c'est pareil
avec chacune l'absence d'amour est autre
avec chacune l'absence d'amour est pareille
(38–39)

The five-line poem plays on sameness and difference, wonderfully multiplied in the French by the difference in the same, when the neutral English "they" as subject has become feminine, necessitating differential forms. Thus a tripled instance of sameness, each to her own, becomes in turn "pareilles," "pareil," and "pareille."

Many of Beckett's translations are competent, but unsurprising and uneventful. Take his early translations of surrealists like Paul Éluard, done for André Breton's special issue of *This Quarter* in 1932, where only some parts shine forth, from a rather dull remainder. In Éluard's "L'univers-solitude," three illustrative lines of the French are rather flat compared to the more interesting English into which the poet has transformed them.

J'admirais descendant vers toi
L'espace occupé par le temps
Nos souvenirs me transportaient

Il te manque beaucoup de place
Pour être toujours avec moi.

&

I admired, descending upon thee
Time in the chariot of space
Our memories transported me

Much room is denied thee
For ever with me.
(82–83)

Often the very brevity of the English, as in the example here,
shows a poetic compression. Take the middle line of Éluard's poem
"A perte de vue dans le sens de mon corps": "Et les passantes ex-
halées par tes recherches obstinées," which Beckett rendered as
"And women that pass in a fume from thy dour questing" (68-69).
Here, the "thy" seems to work better; but later, in Beckett's translations of the epic poems of Rimbaud and Apollinaire, "The Drunken
Boat" and "Zone," Beckett will leave this Quakerish "thee" for a
more ordinary "you," less off-putting to the reader.

To see the quality of the best of these early translations, we have
only to look at the conclusion of Éluard's "Scène," from *La vie
immédiate* of 1932:

Taillée au gré des vents l'eau fait l'éclaboussée
L'éclat du jour s'enflamme aux courbes de la vague
Et dans son corset noir une morte séduit
Les scarabées de l'herbe et des branchages morts.

Parmi tant de passants.

Here is Beckett's own end game:

Playing with the pollen of the breath of the night
Hewn at the hands of the winds the water
Catches up her skirts and the scrolls of wave
Set the spark of dawn aflame

And in her black bodice a corpse seduces
The scarabs of the grass and of the dead boughs

In a so thoroughfare
(76–77)

The expression "In a so thoroughfare" permits the following
through of the visual—the eye rhyme from bough to thorough—
and the ambivalent status of the strange and wonderful word order.
There is so much to see, and what there is, is seen thoroughly. The
contradiction of the deadness with the living mass of persons is what
the branches of the poem shade with such delicacy, after the deliberately strong contrast of the water and the flame, the seduction of
death, and the vitality of death's opposite.

And finally, the end of Éluard's "Confections":

Soleil fatal du nombre des vivants
On ne conserve pas ton coeur.

No less mannered, no less perfect, is Beckett's:

Fatal sun of the quick
One cannot keep thy heart
(90–91)

But it often seems to me that Beckett's singular discoveries in expression come out best in his translations, epic in feeling, of those
long poems in which the grandest poets of our day—the Homers of
our own happenstance—may give the reader, and themselves, their
very best. Of Rimbaud's celebrated "Le bateau ivre," Beckett makes
the finest translation I know, among many. It is a poem of setting out,
as a poet and a boat—sailing on the water of the word, in a realization
of the definition given by the poet René Char of the original *poeisis*:
the making of a craft. The highly crafted stanza in which Rimbaud
bathes in the poem of the sea, literally, is transformed by Beckett into
a liquid fusion, strong in its monosyllabic Anglo-Saxon feeling.

Thenceforward, fused in the poem, milk of stars
Of the sea, I coiled through deeps of cloudless green,

leading to the last lines:

> Where, dimly, they came swaying down,
> Rapt and sad, singly, the drowned
> (95)

So the single drowned man, mad and pensive, turns into a multitude, in a very slow motion, rapt and carried away by thought. In the final rhyme of the stanza, "down . . . drowned," the whole depth of poetry is explored.

Everywhere, echoes are newly fathomed: "herds . . . surf . . . herds . . .":

> J'ai suivi, des mois pleins, pareille aux vacheries
>
> Hystériques, la boule à l'assaut des récifs,
> Sans songer que les pieds lumineux des Maries
> Pussent forcer le muffle aux Océans poussifs.
>
> J'ai heurté, savez-vous? d'incroyables Florides
> Mêlant aux fleurs des yeux de panthères aux peaux
> D'hommes, des arcs-en-ciel tendus comme des brides
> Sous l'horizon des mers, à de glauques troupeaux.

> I have followed months long the maddened herds of the surf
>
> Storming the reefs, mindless of the feet,
> The radiant feet of the Marys that constrain
> The stampedes of the broken-winded Oceans.
>
> I have fouled, be it known, unspeakable Floridas, tangle of
> The flowers of the eyes of panthers in the skins of
> Men and the taut rainbows curbing,
> Beyond the brows of the seas, the glaucous herds.
> (98–99)

For the difficult expression "j'ai heurté, savez-vous?" Beckett's "be it known" replaces any thought of a question. It is not a matter of what Rimbaud seems to be asking: "Can you share in this experience with me?" but rather of a statement in the imperative: "let it be so."

The ways in which Beckett is nonliteral are just the ways in which he is poetic: exaggerating here, displacing the doubling there. For the simple expression "navrantes," in "Les aubes sont navrantes," he gives not the normal "upsetting," but rather: "have broken my heart . . ." Beckett's touch is not just sure; it is often, itself, heart-breaking.

> Mais, vrai, j'ai trop pleuré. Les aubes sont navrantes,
> Toute lune est atroce et tout soleil amer.
> L'âcre amour m'a gonflé de torpeurs enivrantes.
> Oh! que ma quille éclate! Oh! que j'aille à la mer!
>
> ❧
>
> But no more tears. Dawns have broken my heart,
> And every moon is torment, every sun bitterness;
> I am bloated with the stagnant fumes of acrid loving—
> May I split from stem to stern and founder, ah founder!
> (104–5)

Now, every translator knows how impossible it generally is to render with any conviction an "Oh! Oh!" or "O! O!" such as the many desperate (and often desperately dreadful) efforts to translate Baudelaire's famous lines from "A une passante":

> Ô toi que j'eusse aimée! Ô toi qui le savais!

For the repeated "Oh!" of Rimbaud's French, this simple and totally adequate "ah" in English suffices. Even the lowercase makes its point: there is no need to go further. Beckett's understatements are an essential part of his genius.

In Beckett's rendering of Rimbaud's great poem, the quiet of the young Rimbaud's sadness meets its equal:

> Si je désire une eau d'Europe, c'est la flache
> Noire et froide où vers le crépuscule embaumé
> Un enfant accroupi, plein de tristesse, lâche
> Un bateau frêle comme un papillon de mai.
>
> ❧

I want none of Europe's waters unless it be
The cold black puddle where a child, full of sadness,
Squatting, looses a boat as frail
As a moth into the fragrant evening.
(104–5)

The culmination of Beckett's translations of poetry is, I think, his rendering of Guillaume Apollinaire's celebrated "Zone" of 1913, the grand epic. Beckett undertook this task for the publisher Edward Titus, in order to make the money he required to leave France in 1950: it is as moving as it is inventive. None of the moments in Beckett's translation that I shall be considering—moments because, among other things, this zone is a time zone—is at all like any of the many other translations in English.

Some parts are simplified. For the frequent intertwining of such expressions as the Apollinairean "Voilà" and "Il y a," as "Look!" and "there is" with the spectacle of modernity—the poetic astonishment in front of the contemporary universe, which makes this the great beginning poem of modernism—Beckett gives this:

> Tu lis les prospectus les catalogues les affiches qui chantent tout
>   haut
> Voilà la poésie ce matin et pour la prose il y a les journaux
> Il y a les livraisons à 25 centimes pleines d'aventures policières
> Portraits des grands hommes et mille titres divers
>   *₰*
> You read the handbills the catalogues the singing posters
> So much for poetry this morning and the prose is in the papers
> Special editions full of crimes
> Celebrities and other attractions for 25 centimes

And some parts become more complex. In the beginning, the annunciatory shepherdess, "Bergère"—that Eiffel Tower guiding all the bridges—disappears into their herd:

> A la fin tu es las de ce monde ancien
>
> Bergère ô tour Eiffel le troupeau des ponts bêle ce matin
>   *₰*

In the end you are weary of this ancient world

This morning the bridges are bleating Eiffel Tower oh herd
(106-7)

For the famous ascension passage, concerning Christ rising as an
airplane, Beckett gives this:

> Pupille Christ de l'oeil
> Vingtième pupille des siècles il sait y faire
> > Et changé en oiseau ce siècle comme Jésus monte dans l'air
> > Les diables dans les abîmes lèvent la tête pour le regarder
> > Ils disent qu'il imite Simon Mage en Judée
> ❧
> Pupil Christ of the eye
> Twentieth pupil of the centuries it is no novice
> > And changed into a bird this century soars like Jesus
> > The devils in the deeps look up and say they see a
> > Nimitation of Simon Magus in Judea
> (110-11)

Reading the wonderfully witty:

a

Nimitation,

the reader remembers again that "smile's" of Gerard Manley Hopkins, presented in chapter 6.

As his own craft is so understated, Beckett's play on words as vessels comes over as strong as it is humanly simple. Many translators
have stumbled over the following lines:

> Ils crient s'il sait voler qu'on l'appelle voleur
> Les anges voltigent autour du joli voltigeur
> Icare Enoch Élie Apollonius de Thyane
> Flottent autour du premier aéroplane
> ❧
> Craft by name by nature craft they cry
> About the pretty flyer the angels fly

Enoch Elijah Apollonius of Tyana hover
With Icarus round the first airworthy ever
(110–11)

Changing the "voler . . . voleur" to "craft by name by nature craft," and also the "voltigent . . . voltigeur" to "the pretty flyer the angels fly," not only satisfies the rhyming desire in reader and poet, but exploits the English language to its fullest. The "first airworthy ever" cleverly elides any literal mention of the actual plane, stealing it away.

As Thomas Kuhn celebrated the artful science of paradigm shifts, so Apollinaire celebrates the possibility of pronoun shifts, in the center of his astonishing "Zone." He does a trick equally crafted and no less simple, in a celebrated passage alternating personal pronouns from the "tu" to the "je."

> Tu as fait de douloureux et de joyeux voyages
> Avant de t'apercevoir du mensonge et de l'âge
> Tu as souffert de l'amour à vingt et à trente ans
> J'ai vécu comme un fou et j'ai perdu mon temps
> Tu n'oses plus regarder tes mains et à tous moments je voudrais
>   sangloter
> Sur toi sur celle que j'aime sur tout ce qui t'a épouvanté
> ❧
> Grievous and joyous voyages you made
> Before you knew what falsehood was and age
> At twenty you suffered from love and at thirty again
> My life was folly and my days in vain
> You dare not look at your hands tears haunt my eyes
> For you for her I love and all the old miseries
> (116–17)

The translation is heartrending in its closeness to the personal, seen from within and without, no longer making the "tu" into a "thou" but—as it must be when we speak to ourselves, by the quite simple "you." As for the tears haunting my eyes, for the "je voudrais sangloter," Beckett has not only managed to rhyme in English, but to shorten and change to a perfect expression of the "je voudrais sangloter . . . tout ce qui t'a épouvanté," that unspeakable spokenness of grief in "all the old miseries" as no other translator has managed to do.

This greatest of all travel poems ends with what we might see as the ur-image of modernism, the sun cut off at its neck and tipping over for us to stare into a circle of red.

Adieu Adieu

Soleil cou coupé

ಜ

Adieu Adieu

Sun corseless head
(120–21)

This "soleil cou coupé" has seen more ink running than any blood that ever poured from any severed neck. The sound "cou coupé" mocks us like a guillotined cuckoo and yet blazes with drama, providing the visionary verbal shock. The usual translations give just variations of the "sun severed neck." But Beckett's "Sun corseless head" of 1950 leaps from the page to strike the same harsh blow that the beheading itself does, and we hear in the "corseless" or necklace that echo of a corpse so unmistakably marking the end of a beginning. For this 1913 poem was at the beginning of modernism as we know it, and this 1950 translation renders it, and modernism, newly.

But directly before this year of 1950, Beckett's poetic work and the modifications in his poetry, as in his translations of the years in 1948–49, show him coming closer to an involvement in the present and an increased willingness to place some sort of personal expression in his poems. I want to take one translation from that particular period as exemplary, meaningful, and generative.

Take his corrections in French, for example, to an untitled poem beginning "que ferais-je sans ce monde sans visage sans question" ("what would I do without this world faceless incurious") (58–59). Originally, the faces were plural: "visages," indicating a potential changeability absent from the more straightforward singular term "visage." Whether the qualification applies to the self or the world, the singularity brings us closer to the author and to the world than does the plural. We are moving closer in to the world as to the author.

When he is finally multiple, it is along more complex lines and has to do with the generation of the text itself.

The last word of the initial line of the second stanza, "que ferais-je je ferais comme hier comme aujour'hui," was originally "avant-hier," explaining the English: "what would I do what I did yesterday and the day before"—to bring this wondering up to the present makes the same impression of increased nearness as the reducing of the multiple facets to one single face.

So I end by what I am calling a multiple translation in three layers: Beckett's superb translation of René Char's "Courbet: *The Stone Breakers*" makes, as Char makes, a poem of the painting. These are two men from Provence, haunted by the spirit of the place, its melancholy and its gray color, the background for the brightness, as the painter Roger Fry pointed out so long ago. Here is the beginning of Beckett's Provençal lament, "Enueg II":

> world world world world
> and the face grave
> cloud against the evening
> (13)

And from "Malacoda," about the death of his father, the end:

> all aboard all souls half-mast
> aye aye
>
> nay
> (26)

Beckett's translation of Char's Courbet poem has a quiet sense of authority about it:

> "Courbet: *Les Casseurs de cailloux*"
>
> Sable paille ont la vie douce le vin ne s'y brise pas
> Du colombier ils récoltent les plumes
> De la goulotte ils ont la langue avide
> Ils retardent l'orteil des filles
> Dont ils percent les chrysalides

Le sang bien souffert tombe dans l'anecdote de leur légèreté

Nous dévorons la peste du feu gris dans la rocaille
Quand on intrigue à la commune
C'est encore sur les chemins ruinés qu'on est le mieux
Là les tomates des vergers l'air nous les porte au crépuscule
Avec l'oubli de la méchanceté prochaîne de nos femmes
Et l'aigreur de la soif tassée aux genoux

Fils cette nuit nos travaux de poussière
Seront visibles dans le ciel
Déjà l'huile du plomb ressuscite.
☙

"Courbet: *The Stone Breakers*"

Sand straw live softly softly take the wine
Gather the down-drifting dovecot feathers
Parch with the avid water-channel
Stay girls barefoot going

Pierce their chrysalids
Drink lightly carelessly the well suffered blood

We devour the grey fire's pest among the stones
While in the village they plot and plan
The best place still for men is the ruined roads
The tomatoes in the garden are borne to us on the twilight air
And of our women's next spite forgetfulness
And the smart of thirst aching in our knees

Sons this night our labor of dust
Will be visible in the sky
Already the oil rises from the lead again.
(Char 14–15)

Beckett's version privileges the sibilants straight away:

sand
straw

softly
softly

The whispered "s" makes a calm backdrop, soft as the feathers, for
the ritual about to take place. On the basic liquid elements—wine,
water, and blood—the essential actions are performed: the living,
gathering, doing, and drinking. Moreover, the actions to be undertaken are phrased as commands:

live
take
gather
parch
stay
pierce
drink

Both poems move from quiet scene through a noisy contrast: this
labor of men and the chatter of women, to a final celestial transcen-
dence, where work becomes constellation, as so often in Char. If
Beckett's translation has a different flavor from that of Char in its
volume—it moves from the quiet commanding scene to a final starlit
one—it is no less intense in its own working out. The general effect is
the same: the heroic labor of men, like the birthing of women, is the
source of what endures. This is the point of the communion taken
in the poem, in both poems.

As for the two poems in their relation to the canvas that is
their double inspiration, the overlay is triple: Courbet's painting—
in which you see one older man with the stone-breaking instrument
and behind him a younger man with the same instrument—is over-
written by Char's. Now we have an intense viewing of an allegory:
this stone breaking is *man's* work.

As Char's ofttimes translator, as in fact the translator also of this
poem before the Beckett translation was authenticated, I feel a particular personal investment in this canvas, in this poem, and in its
translation. Having translated and given a feminist interpretation
of Char's long poem "Le Visage nuptial," at the end of which the
male stands upright and the female just breathes (Char 28–33), I
can scarcely claim to be reading this text and what it yields under

different management in English as an impersonal witness. Rather, it is my pretext for an aside about the world and the work of the male artist and poet and translator. I notice: on the road the men are working; along the road pass the lovely barefoot girls, nubile and—how shall I put it?—pre-menopausal. At home the women are doing their spiteful gossipy thing, preparing mischief along with the soup, while the man and his son are out sending up signals to the sky.

Under all the layers of paint and French poetry and English poetry here, I am remembering one thing first of all: in Courbet's scene, the man has one young man behind him, presumably his son—or, if they are two models, as seems to have been the case, posing as his son. There is no visual proof of their being related, only a logical guess. It is rather a case like the celebrated one of the two Van Gogh shoes treated by Martin Heidegger as obviously a pair and by Jacques Derrida as being not necessarily a pair (Derrida 257-382), and by Meyer Schapiro as indicative of Heidegger's thinking. These two figures might, partaking of a long tradition, simply connote two stages of life and work, for all the viewer knows. And as for verbal guesswork, in fact the French word *fils* is ambiguous, referring to one or more sons, or then to many *fils*, or threads: *les fils*. This tapestry of men is opposite to the tapestry of women, to their chatter and their essentially private weave. Char, thinking of the canvas, is thinking of man and boy, as father and son. He is privileging the work of men, as I think he always did. Beckett—not remembering the canvas, perhaps, or then reinterpreting it—writes *fils* in the plural, as "Sons."

Does any of this matter? Intensely so, I believe, although only as an image. To me, it indicates that the memory or the reading has the power to multiply, like so many night stars among which the work will rise splendid like oil—like the oil of the painting as well as the essence of poetry—and will be forever triumphant over dust. Whether or not this is Beckett's intention is not the point here: my point is the impression made upon the reader, which is in fact the only position from which we can speak.

I see, then, this particular layer of translation as a laying on of hands, a multiplication of the actual into the virtual. So in this thick and personal reading, Courbet's work about work becomes first a heroic venture in the Provençal reading of it, transforming the base into the essential and the transcendent. And then, in Beckett's rereading, the painting's work is multiplied into the work of generations, to be carried on, father to sons, downward into the generations and from then on upward. So Beckett's translation finds itself or makes itself, stressing Char's own upward movement, like his volume called *Retour amont*, that return of the river upstream, and the return of the poet to the source. The two poems are about generation, of the family, of the text, and of the work of reading the road and the sky. And so our reading of Beckett, whatever course it follows, in whatever direction seems the most promising—whether of his poetry, his prose, or his translations—seems always to increase our own original intent, and to intensify our own perception, of work on the canvas, on the road, on the self, and on the word. Isn't that what poetry is about?

VIII. *Shakespeare, Keats, and Yeats, by Bonnefoy*

Translation becomes the struggle of a language with its own nature, at the very core of its being, the quickening point of its growth.
—Yves Bonnefoy, *Shakespeare and the French Poet*, 222

WHEN, MANY YEARS ago, I first heard Yves Bonnefoy read his poems and those of François Villon, what struck me most was the way his voice often broke, quivered if you like, in the middle of the verses. Now, all this time later, reading his essays on the translation of Shakespeare, that memory comes back all the more strongly. Speaking of the Shakespearean line, Bonnefoy stresses the great breaks in the words, not just of the English language but of the great dramatist's *parole* (a distinction he insists on, for the specific individual use by each poet, that which betrays and portrays presence). These breaks "boldly expose . . . a field of perceptions, worries, values, conflicts, rifts, passions, which constitute for Shakespeare the poetic recovery of existence" (*Poet* 268).

The subject arises again when Bonnefoy is opposing a suggestion that Shakespeare's drama should be translated with a Claudelian verset (too long, too abundant, too optimistic, says Bonnefoy), stressing instead its "torment." "It identifies with the voice, breaks with its anguish, picks up with its newfound hopes, hardens when it might have come undone in the distress of the moment"(227). To ignore the torment is to leave behind the essential, the part that breaks, questions, gives the characters their roundness, as Bonnefoy puts it, and with it, there disappears the ambiguity of authorial genius.

Ambiguity and question: two elements important for the French poet. What most perturbs him in some translations of *Hamlet*, for example, is that some French translators "abandon the space of the question" that there always is (229). Bonnefoy seems always haunted by space and spaces. . . . In French poetry as such, he treasures— I think the word not too strong—the space between words. Spatial form, you can feel him thinking, as in the title of the important and relevant work of his close friend the critic Joseph Frank. Often that space is the space of finitude, again a break, this time in being itself: "it's in the current that passes from the lure of timelessness to the experience of finitude that I want to follow Shakespeare" (264). Bonnefoy's translations of the plays have an evident mortal melancholy, quite the opposite feeling from Gide's translations, which Bonnefoy describes as seeing the theater through a windowpane. That very transparency, we are given to surmise, must rule out any affect, thus reducing the very power of Shakespeare so appealing to contemporary readers (25).

Bonnefoy recounts the way in which he first began his translations of the great English poet. Pierre Jean Jouve had asked him to translate *Julius Caesar* for an edition of the Elizabethan poet in preparation by Pierre Leyris, the renowned translator of Gerard Manley Hopkins and James Joyce. After he submitted his translation, instantly approved by Leyris, he was included in the project. Leyris, who was translating all the sonnets himself, died at ninety-three. Jouve had translated the entire corpus of sonnets, and Bonnefoy, after translating many of the plays, rendered sixty of the sonnets into French. So we have translations by both Jouve and Bonnefoy, completely different in tone and purpose, playing out an entirely different drama on the stage that is, of necessity, a mental one (268).

In his French translations of Shakespeare's sonnets, in the Collection *Poésie* (published by Gallimard) of 1969, Jouve speaks of his work on the poems, in which, as he puts it, "discourse often supplants the image" (Shakespeare, *Sonnets* 14). Less visual than verbal, then, the prose translations of these sonnets were never intended to be in verse. Jouve wanted to "discover a French form which would be less ambitious but just as carefully worked," depending on an interior organization and a scansion in prose. He took as a model Mallarmé's translations of Edgar Allan Poe, according himself the liberty of reinforcing the colors of the words, suppressing articles and pronouns, and using inversions to signal the "relative distance between ourselves and Shakespeare," to whom he wanted to "erect a modern monument" (19).

Bonnefoy, for whom "poetry is the constitution of a sacred order," maintains that we must translate Shakespeare or any other poet into verse, or risk losing the essence and the point of the poetic work (*Poet* 233–36). His "impassioned choice of poetry," in the case of Shakespeare, involves free verse and a variable number of lines in the sonnet, not the classic twelve, but rather seventeen or eighteen lines, keeping to the four parts, and the shorter part at the end, but exempting himself as a poet from the procrustean bed of convention. In all his poetic translations, he admits and, I feel, even cherishes "the gap between the person one is and the person one admires. I have not tried to render the singular rhythms of Yeats into French: nor would I dream of trying to copy the verbal music of the Elizabethan poet" (255).

To correspond with his four parts maintained, I shall take as examples four poems—poems of lust and madness, loss and love, of age and death, interior richness of soul and thought—and shall stress on that basis the power of poetry for survival. The French poet has stated his wish to follow the English poet from timelessness to finitude and the choice of these poems follows also that current.

In translation, particularly from the insuperable grandeur of a Shakespeare sonnet, it is often a question of substituting a power endemic to the target language for what cannot be attained directly. Bonnefoy points out that the English language is "subordinate to the external object, which is something English allows. Nouns fade before the real presence of things, which stand starkly before us in the actual process of becoming" (218). For example, in sonnet 146, beginning:

> Poor soul, the center of my sinful earth,
> Lord of these rebel powers that thee array,
> Why does thou pine within and suffer dearth,
> Painting thy outward walls so costly gay?

Here, the walls, appearing so suddenly in the fourth verse, loom up inescapably before us, as if in their fresh paint. Their visuality is so strong as to triumph in the first instance over any simply metaphorical thought of waste and uselessness. Jouve's translation follows literally, with "Pauvre âme," while Bonnefoy's at once personalizes the very beginning and strengthens the centrality of the opening by cutting the initial exclamation loose from its surroundings, in a brief first verse, followed by a triplet "de . . . de . . . des," again stressing the centrality, before the metaphoric shift to the "dehors peints," as opposed to the inner anguish. The outer trappings are, in their turn, less stark (and that is indeed the perfect word) and less concretely pictured than the walls of the original. So that in this case, the visual power of the English stanza is compensated for by the personal exclamation "Ma pauvre âme" and its terrible centrality.

> Ma pauvre âme, le centre
> De ma terre coupable; et de toujours la proie
> Des puissances rebelles qui t'assaillent!
> Pourquoi céler tant d'angoisse et de soif
> Sous des dehors peints de couleurs si gaies?
> (Bonnefoy, "Douze sonnets" 12)

To continue with this sonnet, another of Bonnefoy's remarks on translating from English is apposite. In that language, he says, "the word is an opening, it is all surface; and in French it is a closing, it is all depth" (*Poet*, 220). French abhors the pun so familiar and beloved in English, particularly at this period—famously exemplified in John Donne's play on his name and his death: "Donne/done . . ." By extension, then, the French poet has us think, in English, of a mirror, and in French, of a globe. This sonnet ends with a triple wordplay on feeding, as in the action of the worms upon the corpse, and on death, in each case varying the word played upon to yield three different modulations: "Fed . . . feed . . . feeds" and right after, "Death . . . dead . . . dying."

> Within be fed, without be rich no more.
> So shalt thou feed on death, that feeds on men,
> And death once dead, there's no more dying then.

In French, the play of the words "nourish" and "die" responds to this, in its own triple variation, twice: "Nourrie . . . nourriras . . . nourrit . . . La mort . . . morte . . . mourir," while the intense personalization sensed at the outset of "my soul" instead of "poor soul" reappears: "tu te nourriras . . . Tu n'auras plus à craindre."

> Le temps mortel. Que ce soit au dedans
> Que tu es bien nourrie et riche, non au dehors!
>
> Ainsi faisant, tu te nourriras de la mort
> Qui se nourrit des hommes. Et la mort morte,
> Tu n'auras plus à craindre de mourir.
> ("Douze sonnets" 12)

Jouve's version feels a bit heavy alongside this, ending:

> Ainsi tu te nourriras de la Mort, qui d'hommes se nourrit;
> la Mort une fois morte, rien ne sera plus mort.
> (*Sonnets* 172)

Bonnefoy notices in the English poem the way in which the verse is an extension of the tonic stress "that is the soul of each English word; it begins with the very first word in a line" (*Poet*, 260). Illustrating this is the celebrated sonnet 73 about age and its desiccating effect, starting off with the stress on the leading term "time," in alliterative junction with "that" and "thou," so strengthened on all sides:

> That time of year thou mayst in me behold
> When yellow leaves, or none, or few, do hang
> Upon those boughs which shake against the cold,
> Bare ruined choirs, where late the sweet birds sang.

Bonnefoy's version, unlike Jouve's literalizing "tu peux le voir," puts the stronger element in his first verse first, before "ce moment de l'année," the act of seeing, and again personalizes and intensifies it, not just "thou may'st" and "in me thou see'st" but a command, moreover finding the verb "contempler," in which the sound of "time" is present, as in the French "temps":

Contemple en moi ce moment de l'année
Où les feuilles des arbres ont jauni,
Puis sont tombées; et peu pendent encore
A leurs branches qui s'ébouriffent dans le froid:
Chapelles nues en ruines,
Où les chantres, ce furent tard des chants d'oiseaux.
("Douze sonnets" 6)

So stands an example of his liberal approach toward the addition of lines; and in this case, the emphasis lies on the "chapelles nues en ruines," standing alone and bare. So strong is this feeling that there is no need of "sweet" for the birds: their song is just that. The poem continues with its extra line in the center, adding a repose and the eyelids, not just eyelids, but the "paupières de tout," rounding out the idea—that force of the French poem as Bonnefoy never ceases to point out.

Contemple en moi la journée qui s'achève,
La trace à l'Occident que le soleil laisse
Mais que bientôt les ombres de la nuit,
Cette autre mort, effaceront, qui cousent
Pour le repos les paupières de tout.
(6)

And then the ending, where the alliteration of the concluding sadness—"love . . . love . . . leave . . . long"—in its mirror effect cannot be exactly found, but must be transferred and transformed:

In me thou see'st the twilight of such day
As after sunset fadeth in the west;
Which by and by black night doth take away,
In me thou see'st the glowing of such fire,
Death's second self, that seals up all in rest.
In me thou see'st the glowing of such fire,
That on the ashes of his youth doth lie,
As the deathbed whereon it must expire,
Consumed with that which it was nourished by.
This thou perceiv'st, which makes thy love more strong,
To love that well which thou must leave ere long.

In the French poetry version, the solution Bonnefoy finds is a triple play on loving in its various tenses and its knowingness:

> Contemple en moi le rougeoiement d'un feu
> Qui gît parmi les cendres de sa jeunesse,
> Ce lit de mort sur lequel il lui faut
> Expirer, de par l'ardeur même qui l'a nourri
>
> Contemple, et contempler fasse ton amour
> Plus fort, d'avoir aimé, d'avoir su aimer
> Ce que dans peu de temps il te faudra perdre.
> (6)

The repetition of the contemplation ("contempler," so "temps . . . temps" we hear), and the extension of the act of loving into the past and the knowing past as well as into the necessary future of contemplation is as moving an effect as could be achieved.

Finally, sonnet 129 about "the expense of spirit" is translated in a daringly choppy version, in place of the long Shakespearean line, as an illustration of the dangers of such expense, such waste, such shame, with the choppiness emphasizing the violence of the verse. This is reminiscent of Bonnefoy's remark about the great breaks in the words of Shakespeare "that boldly expose . . . a field of perceptions, worries, values, conflicts, rifts, passions, which constitute for Shakespeare the poetic recovery of existence" (*Poet* 268). Here he uses the "force vitale" instead of the multiple-sensed English "spirit" about the translation of which Bonnefoy is so expansive. The vital force is just right for what is shamefully expended, compared with the literalism of Jouve's "l'esprit dispersé dans un abîme de honte":

> Th'expense of spirit in a waste of shame
> Is lust in action; and till action, lust
> Is perjured, murderous, bloody, full of blame,
> Savage, extreme, rude, cruel, not to trust;
> Enjoyed no sooner but despised straight:
> Past reason hunted; and no sooner had,
> Past reason hated, as a swallowed bait,
> On purpose laid to make the taker mad:

Mad in pursuit, and in possession so;
Had, having, and in quest to have, extreme;
A bliss in proof, and proved, a very woe;
Before, a joy proposed; behind, a dream.
All this the world well knows; yet none knows well
To shun the heaven that leads men to this hell.
(*Sonnets* 155)

ਕ

La luxure: naufrage, en abîme de honte,
De la force vitale. Rien qu'en pensée
Elle est parjure, meurtrière, elle répand
Coupablement le sang, elle est sauvage,
Excessive, brutale et cruelle, traîtresse,

Et méprisée si tôt que satisfaite,
Follement poursuivie mais follement
Haïe, le hameçon qu'on a dans la bouche
Fait pour que l'esprit sombre, par la douleur.
("Douze sonnets" 9)

One of the most successful plays in the French version is the variation on the idea of madness, picking up on "l'esprit sombre," where
the English "spirit" is finally acknowledged, and where the repetition of "follement . . . follement . . . insensée . . . rage" illustrates
Bonnefoy's general remark about the power of poetic form, where
each line leads necessarily to another, and the memory works its own
seductive web, drawing the reader into the poem: "the line of verse,
which can be written or heard only in the light of another line already
encountered or to come" (*Poet* 244).

Et insensée à vouloir comme à prendre,
Rage de qui a eu, qui possède, qui cherche,
Désirée, un délice, éprouvée, un malheur,
Attendue, une joie, passée, l'ombre d'un songe,

Et cela, qui ne le sait pas? Mais qui sait se garder
De ce ciel qui voue l'homme à tout cet enfer?
("Douze sonnets" 9)

The final form of interrogation, only implicit in the original, feels far stronger than Jouve's simple statement "ce que le monde sait."

The poet lives on in the poem: here Bonnefoy takes up Shakespeare's sonnet 107 about living on and turns living into survival, makes a short line of disappearance, visualizing the act of leaving, and, finally, by personalizing the English poet yet again, makes him live on, in French:

> Now with the drops of this most balmy time
> My love looks fresh, and Death to me subscribes,
> Since, spite of him, I'll live in this poor rhyme,
> While he insults o'er dull and speechless tribes:
> And thou in this shalt find thy monument,
> When tyrants' crests and tombs of brass are spent.
>
> ❧
>
> Et mon amour a des airs de fraîcheur
> Dans la rosée de ce temps bienheureux,
> Et la mort même renonce à me soumettre,
> Puisque je survivrai dans ce pauvre poème
> Quand elle insultera de son mépris
> Les foules sans ressort et sans paroles.
>
> Toi, mes vers te seront ton mémorial
> Quand auront disparus
> Les cimiers des tyrans et les tombes de bronze.
> ("Douze sonnets" 8)

Some of Bonnefoy's translations of Keats (*Keats et Leopardi: Quelques traductions nouvelles*, 2000) illustrate, even startlingly, his remark about the tonic stress "that is the soul of each English word" and begins with the first word in a verse. The opening of "Bright Star" reads:

> Bright star; would I were steadfast as thou art—
> Not in lone splendour hung aloft the night

So that the double accent on "bright star" has to come over into French as doubly stressed, then followed by the mighty phrase: "splendour hung aloft," both these elements difficult to render in another language: that stress and that loftiness. Here is Bonnefoy's answer, which takes three lines for the two—characteristic of his translations, generally more extensive than the original, a visual surprise in itself, this outer shape. But the inner or felt shape is what matters:

> Etoile, tant de feux! Comme toi, que n'ai-je
> Constance, paix, mais non pour veiller seul
> Dans la splendeur des cimes de la nuit
> (Bonnefoy, *Keats* 10–11)

Since in French any equivalent for "bright" would scarcely give the dazzle of the English, those "tant de feux!" and their exclamation point, added in the translation, reach at giving the equivalent. As for the "hung aloft," its celestial suspension is rendered like mountain summits, bringing in a different visual landscape; again, the outer scene is changed in image, but the metaphoric splendor is retained— what I am calling its inner shape.

The same is true of Keats's celebrated "Ode on a Grecian Urn," translated as "A une urne grecque," so that instead of the double play of "on"—as in "about" and "written on"—the French version simply dedicates itself to that container whose surface holds so much. The repeated questions of the English, as if tapping out some melody that will recur in the "Heard melodies are sweet, but those unheard / Are sweeter," sound a different tone in the French, following the first questions by a statement:

> What men or gods are these? What maidens loth?
> What mad pursuit? What struggle to escape?
> What pipes and timbrels? What wild ecstasy?
> ❧
> Et qui sont-ils, ces jeunes gens, ces dieux,
> Qui, ces filles qu les refusent? Poursuites folles,
> Luttes pour échapper à l'étreinte, et toujours,
> Ces flûtes, ces tambourins, cette joie sauvage.
> (*Keats* 28–29)

Again, we notice the greater number of lines in the French, but more importantly, the sobering statement in the place of the always increasing energy of the Keatsian question: "What . . . ? What . . . ? What . . . ? What . . . ? What . . . ? What . . . ?" For the French mind, this would sound like frenzy, not simple energy— thus the statement without interrogation, in which, all the same, the increase of emotion is marked by the "toujours"—*always* these, these, these . . . Instead of a mimetic parroting of the "What . . . ? What . . . ?" the resolution is a seemingly calmer poem, with its energy directed inside: "always." The exterior form of the Bonnefoy translations always looks different from the English form, far longer: this is its "heard" form. And the poem feels, always, like a Bonnefoy poem: you could scarcely mistake it for another poet's rendering. But inside, the English poet's spirit remains, if unheard at first:

> Heard melodies are sweet, but those unheard
> Are sweeter . . .
>
> ❧
>
> Douce la mélodie qu'on entend, mais plus douce encore
> L'autre, l'inentendue . . .
> (28–29)

We are fortunate in having Yves Bonnefoy's preface to his translations of Yeats, not only as a guide to his own choices, but as a meditation on the translating work as he conceives of it. It is, from all points of view, an optimistic conception of the art of translation. That it should be, in this case, a question of Yeats is significant in this optimistic light, since the Irish poet manifests—according to Bonnefoy—a kind of momentary but nevertheless fully rounded joy that is characteristic only of Shakespeare before or after him, in the English language. And that kind of experience, Bonnefoy maintains, is just what can be rendered in another speech: "The Yeatsean reflection has always something universal, so independent of this or that kind of tongue, like these books near the fire in the house while the snow is falling, that it can almost relive more fully in other words than those of the English language" (Yeats 27). What matters, and deeply, is the experience of a full poetic dimension that manifests itself here, that dimension "misrecognized in our societies, refused or repressed" (10). I want to make a claim for the truest translation as *recognition*. But in any case, Bonnefoy's courageous claim about translation as interpretation, explication, even *explicitation* has to be considered. In the matter of Yeats—as with many poets and painters Bonnefoy loves and comments upon, and as is the case in his own poetry—the poetic attitude is itself what seems at once clearest and perhaps most embattled: so it is what has to be defended.

In "Sailing to Byzantium," following Bonnefoy's lead, we may see "a poem which asks you to flee from life, and the alternative it offers, and that we find quickly, ill-disguised in an Ideal, badly repressed, never forgotten, the thing quite simply here" (10). As elsewhere, Bonnefoy salutes, with a frequency we grow to appreciate precisely as it emphasizes the nowness that every translation requires, the "hic et nunc"—whatever proves to be here and now, the things that incarnate presence. That counts, not just the words in their own interrelations with each other, but the *Ding an Sich*, in and of the natural world, has to be caught and portrayed, so as not to be betrayed. "The true object of Yeats is the being of flesh and blood, these '*birds in the trees*'" that are not of bronze, that will, indeed perish unless we catch them in the net of our interpretation, explication, explanation even. These are, on occasion, "symbols, but in order to stir up the ground of what is lived, not to substitute for it the worlds of dream" (19).

We elucidate, explain, and explicate, at the risk, of course, of spelling out the ellipsis of the poem into the non-ellipsis of our own words. Unlike Mallarmé, of whose poetry Bonnefoy has spoken, it seems to me, better than any other, Yeats is "negligent," repeating words without any special meaning to the repetition. In so doing, he brings startlingly to life with a rapid luminosity like a lightning flash a few moments that illuminate and transfigure, in Bonnefoy's words, a passionate adhesion to the present, before the intrusion of all "The Sorrow of Love" and the intense nostalgia, for which Yeats is so celebrated:

> They came like swallows and like swallows went,

says Yeats of some poets as if they were representative of transience itself. As perhaps they are. But not so Yeats. The bees buzzing and the modest rows of beans that cause Yeats to "arise and go now, and go to Innisfree" (38–39) set in motion a quite extraordinary reality for the reader. This land is precisely the one that is never waste, the one of T. S. Eliot, which Bonnefoy represents as "full of signs opaque and dead" (Yeats 23), unlike Yeats's living symbols in a living land.

It is crucial to portray these moments lest we betray them. So that the vexed and ceaselessly vexing notion of fidelity is, for the French poet and translator, wider than a simple reference to surface saying. It is a personalized rendering, and indeed Bonnefoy's notion of translation is that to interpret is to implicate yourself personally, because of the choices you have to make and, thus, oblige yourself to know yourself better—that is, to change, to become (*Poet* 29).

As an example, Bonnefoy takes his interpretation, necessarily a choice, of the initial word of the final and famous stanza from "Among School Children" (88–89):

> Labour is blossoming or dancing . . .

Now, of course in English, this *labour* is both work and the process of giving birth. The latter interpretation is what he has chosen to represent. And in so doing, he has represented what was most important for him:

> But it was not without feeling myself obliged by this very decision to retrace my thoughts, my intuitions fallen asleep here and there, to reflect on poetry, to restretch my own cords. Which is to say that my experiences, my memories, my nostalgias, have been invested, a little more even, in my reading of another. (Yeats 30)

On this choice, it seems to me, hangs a world of things to be said about translation itself. That often we—as poets, translators, readers—recognize in the rendering of a single word the explanation of an entire thought, poem, way of being, world. That the singularity of this choice leaps out from the text to tell us something we might not have known. That here the bringing to birth and light an entire world is the point of the work as of the word. So Bonnefoy's translations of Yeats and of his "labour" seem a crucial representation of his own credence in work, in that kind of giving birth that poetic struggle is for him.

What Bonnefoy has done for Yeats in French fulfills, to my ears and eyes, his purpose in translating: "This work I would like to have

living in our language . . ." (Yeats 7). I want to examine some individual parts of the birth-giving process that I, too, take translation
to be, relying often on a detail that seems to deliver the poem after,
or through, the labor of translation, speaking, while doing so, of the
translator as poet. To that labor, I will be returning.

Now as a poet and an essayist, Bonnefoy is known for his insistence on presence; on the living detail as opposed to dead conceptu-
alizations. And just so, in his translations of Yeats, that is what comes
through with greatest clarity. "Down by the Salley Gardens," with
its so familiar and lightly distressed refrain of love meeting and then
lost, changes the original "my love" and the third-person "she" to
a startling second-person familiar address, in the attempt to bring it
closer to hand. The translation illustrates how very difficult it is to
maintain the same light tone in French; the intimate address works in
that direction, even as the nostalgic distancing loses its force: "she"
and "I" feel sadder than "you," which might somehow indicate the
beloved is still in earshot or poem-shot. . . . But here it is:

> Down by the salley gardens my love and I did meet;
> She passed the salley gardens with little snow-white feet.
> She bid me take love easy, as the leaves grow on the tree;
> But I, being young and foolish, with her would not agree.
> . . . .
> She bid me take life easy, as the grass grows on the weirs;
> But I was young and foolish, and now am full of tears.
>   ❧
> Au bas des jardins de saules je t'ai rencontrée, mon amour.
> Tu passais les jardins de saules d'un pied qui est comme neige.
> Tu me dis de prendre l'amour simplement, ainsi que poussent les
>   feuilles,
> Mais moi j'etais jeune et fou et n'ai pas voulu te comprendre.
> . . . .
> Tu me dis de prendre la vie simplement, comme l'herbe pousse sur
>   la levée,
> Mais moi j'etais jeune et fou et depuis lors je te pleure.
> (Yeats 34–35)

The same technique applies to the Ronsard/Yeats lament about
time and warning to the not-so-loving lady, "When You Are Old"

(modeled on Ronsard's "Quand tu seras vieille . . ."). The lady now nodding near the fire will be mourning, in Yeats:

> Murmur, a little sadly, how Love fled:
> And paced upon the mountains overhead
> And hid his face amid a crowd of stars.
> (44)

In Bonnefoy's rendering, the old lady addresses Love directly as her love, in a murmur all the more intimate for being "à voix basse":

> Et dis-toi, un peu triste, à voix basse: "Amour,
> Tu as donc fui, tu as erré sans fin sur la montagne,
> Tu t'es caché dans l'innombrable étoile."
> (5)

In my judgment, the second of these attempts is far more successful, perhaps because the Yeatsian personification of "Love . . . his face" is already set in a distance that has not the same nostalgia, only a rather mythical/mystical element: a far more removed address that the intimate "toi . . . tu" actually brings into felt presence. Following along these lines, but pushing presence as far as absolute identification, Yeats's "Lake Isle of Innisfree," where his determination to "live alone in the bee-loud glade" becomes "je vivrai seul, devenu le bruit des abeilles" (38–39), as if the loud buzz about his ears were actually to have absorbed him into itself. This is self-discovery with an intensity all the more surprising in the step from hearing to being.

The other most noticeable technique is Bonnefoy's frequent full stop, bringing the sentences to a halt instead of Yeats's long continuities. In a sense, the poem in French is choppier but gets its generally desolating point across perhaps even more strongly. In "The Second Coming," for the celebrated lament held together with commas and semicolons, Bonnefoy will bring the words and thought to a full stop, thus in fact playing out the way things do *not* hold together:

> Things fall apart; the centre cannot hold;
> Mere anarchy is loosed upon the world,
> The blood-dimmed tide is loosed, and everywhere

The ceremony of innocence is drowned
(60)

And the sentence continues from there, still lamenting as it goes. In French, the full stops abound, so that the isolation of things, persons, words, bears in itself the lament of separation, in fact, the threat of semantic anarchy. The sentence goes off alone.

The poet mourns:

Tout se disloque. Le centre ne peut tenir.
L'anarchie se dechaîne sur le monde
Comme une mer noircie de sang: partout
On noie les saints élans de l'innocence.
(61)

The same technique holds true for "Leda and the Swan," for which Bonnefoy's opening renders the first line as dramatic as Yeats's colon:

A sudden blow: the great wings beating still . . .

And Bonnefoy:

Le heurt d'un vent. De grandes ailes battent . . . (81)

The fortune of the French here is that those "ailes" permit the French poet to find, at the summit of the poem, the heroine, "Elle," three times repeating those great wings, haunted and crushed, lifted and made legendary by them. So for Yeats's

And Agamemnon dead.
                    Being so caught up,
So mastered by the brute blood of the air,
Did she put on his knowledge with his power
Before the indifferent beak could let her drop?
(82)

Bonnefoy first triply salutes Leda: "Elle . . . Elle . . . elle" and then, as that indifferent beak lets her drop, reduces the "elle" to a simple letter: "l"—in "*l*'eût laissée choir"— the trace only of that other "aile."

> Et Agammenon mort.
>   Elle emportée,
> Elle écrasée par le sang brut de l'air,
> Prit-elle au moins sa science avec sa force
> Avant qu'indifférent le bec l'eût laissée choir?
> (83)

Equally true of "The Circus Animals' Desertion" is this breaking up of the Yeatsian continuing sentence into Bonnefoy's full stops:

> Maybe at last, being but a broken man,
> I must be satisfied with my heart, although
>
>   ⁊⊸
>
> Peut-être qu'à la fin, vieux comme je suis,
> Je dois me contenter de mon coeur. Et pourtant
> (178–79)

But indeed the greatest leap in these translations occurs in just the poem from which Bonnefoy takes his example of interpretation, that "labour" he interprets as childbirth, rather than simple work. The last stanza of "Among School Children" is in question here, and at risk: the triumph is worth lingering over a moment. For the third element in Bonnefoy's giving birth to the poem of Yeats is concretized directly in the stanza beginning with that "Labour" that blossoms and sways the length of the stanza. And here we see exactly the opposite from the separation of parts that Bonnefoy occasionally uses for dramatic effect. This stanza, and the whole poem with it, blossoms through its own work and birthing in English ("Labour is blossoming . . . nor beauty born . . ."), made concrete by the abundance of the letter "b" in its fullness:

> Labour is blossoming or dancing where
> The body is not bruised to pleasure soul.
> Nor beauty born out of its own despair,
> Nor blear-eyed wisdom out of midnight oil.

O chestnut-tree, great-rooted blossomer,
Are you the leaf, the blossom, or the bole?
O body swayed to music, O brightening glance,
How can we know the dancer from the dance?

ಜ

L'enfantement fleurit ou se fait danse
Si le corps, ce n'est plus ce que meurtrit l'âme,
Ni la beauté le fruit de sa propre angoisse,
Ni la sagesse l'ocil cerné des nuits de veille.
O chataîgnier, souche, milliers de fleurs,
Es-tu le tronc, la fleur ou le feuillage?
O corps que prend le rythme, ô regard, aube,
C'est même feu le danseur et la danse.
(90–91)

For the French poet, this "enfantement," or birth, passes through exactly the same stages of a consonant, but here it is, rather than the "b" of Yeats's blossoming birth, the "f" of the "enfantement" and the foliage and chestnut blossoms, that profusion of flowers ("milliers de fleurs"), and, finally, the fire all this richness leads to. So whereas the solution of the question in the last line—"C'est même feu" ("it is the same fire")—startles at first sight, once it is thought through, it carries the double meaning into the single and unitary fire of motion and performer, work and creation. Rather than a separation of elements, it is now the assured bringing together of what is, in English, a question—in fact, the Yeatsian question so memorable and cited everywhere as the archetypical Yeats query:

O body swayed to music, O brightening glance,
How can we know the dancer from the dance?

First, Bonnefoy transforms the "brightening glance," relying on the power of the dawn and the comma to settle the increase in light by natural means:

O regard, aube

And then he unites the whole:

O corps que prend le rythme, ô regard, aube,
C'est même feu le danseur et la danse.

Whatever one might think of the liberties taken with the number of lines, with the various suppressions and lengthenings, with what some find a heavy touch overlying the gentle folksong quality of the Irish poet, it seems to me that Bonnefoy brings a new kind of vitality to the world of Yeats, and, through the labor, gives birth to a French Yeats recognizably Bonnefoy's and, through this double portrait, in no way betrayed.

Coda: Surrealism as Surprise

SURREALISM WANTS TO be, has been, and always was about surprises. André Breton used to marvel at Tristan Tzara's not having the words to ask for cigarettes in a tobacco store, and he himself declared how you can perfectly well say *farewell* to your beloved whom you are delighted to be greeting after a long absence. He lamented also how he always spoke least well of what he most loved.

These "mistakes" or inappropriate reactions and their upsets of our rational and habitual ways of thinking and speaking exemplify one of the more crucial parts of the surrealist enterprise. If the very being of its most intimate poetics is based on this kind of paradox, might not our best response as translators be paradoxical in nature? Might we not find ourselves experiencing a necessary first step of losing, perhaps both our way and wits, as we move toward a participatory place of surrealist poetry and poetics?

These breaks in logic and in our reaction form our anxiety points. They can occur in some major places, like titles, and some other stressed moments, like the beginnings and endings of poems. My preface to the translation of Breton's *L'Amour fou* as *Mad Love* concluded with an avowal of impossibility:

> To translate such a classic in the sure knowledge of failure is—
> perhaps—to make an impossible gesture of gratitude to a work and

an author of primary significance for us all. It is really a gesture, all these years later, of our own mad love. (*Mad Love*, xvii)

I wrote that in January 1987, delighting in a sort of public admission of pre-failure. I now feel the relevance of Adorno's statement: "The only true thoughts are those who do not grasp their own meaning" (Graham 229). Something about a necessary slippage within the text seems to be the oddly useful point. It is as if a whole congeries of uncertainties were to spring up and crowd around the very idea of translation.

Breton himself leads us toward such uncertainty in the opening of *L'Amour fou*, where the very first word forms an impossibility of translation: "BOYS." They are nameless actors in the text, but what an enormously awkward word. I had to leave that awkwardness and the word "BOYS." Of course it exists in French, as so differently in English. That signally hard beginning says something like: "Come, I dare you to do anything with me." We can't translate it back into French, to give "Jeunes hommes" or, even worse, "Garçons." So we leave it right there: *plunk*.

Breton's opening is very like the impossible and awkward "nothing," the "Rien" that begins Mallarmé's great toast to nothingness, salvation, and everything imaginable in his short poem "Salut." It has been so diversely explained, precisely because of that impossible opening that opens so much, like a kind of salvation: *salut* or, then, a greeting, such as the kind previously used in the first discussion of translation and interior shaping. In the previous discussion, I stressed the deliberate awkwardness of Mallarmé's opening "eyes," those impossible "Yeux" opening and closing off his "Le Pitre châtié," central to my chapter 4. This was a play of extreme verbal difficulty, for the drastically non-mellifluous pronunciation in the French goes against everything we are accustomed to in French poetry. This, too, was an opening on surprise . . . on which also I wish to close.

For a different reason entirely, another surprising and well-nigh impossible rendering arises in Breton's poem called "Vigilance":

Je vois les arêtes du soleil
A travers l'aubépine de la pluie

for which I gave, hesitatingly:

> I see the ridges of the sun
> Through the hawthorn of the rain.
> (Breton, *Poems* 79)

Of course there was no way of getting those "arêtes" or fish bones up to the sun, no way of having them sparkle on the hawthorn, no way—at least I did not find one—of evoking the Proust who had been responsible, in the first place, for the hawthorn.

The poem ends:

> Je ne touche plus que le coeur des choses je tiens le fil
> ⁊
> I touch nothing but the heart of things I hold the thread (79)

And somehow that upbeat ending seemed to hold the poem together, all its contradictory elements gathering force from their opposition.

The technique of anaphora is surely the most visible way of holding the poem together. A singularly famous example is that of "L'Union libre," or "Free Union," with its apostrophe to his beloved, "Ma femme à . . . ," repeated at the outset of many lines, as a litanic invocation the length of the very long love poem. Part of its being well-known arises from its having been recirculated for various women, and yet always feeling fresh. Since this was already its first line, our first step—the first time I translated it with a friend for publication—was a clunker:

> Woman of mine [!] (49)

A mortification, inevitably taken up in the *Norton Anthology*, as is or as was. I have now removed the poem from the volume, rather than leave the thoughtless initial translation. For the 2002 publication of *Surrealist Love Poems*, in which this poem is retranslated with Patricia Terry, we gave "My love." This affection seemed to be less possessive, more celebratory of what was really meant.

My love whose hair is woodfire
Her thoughts heat lightning
Her hourglass waist an otter in the tiger's jaws my love
Her mouth a rosette bouquet of stars of the highest magnitude

My love of savannah eyes
Of eyes of water to drink in prison
Eyes of wood always to be chopped
Eyes of water level earth and air and fire
(Caws, *Surrealist* 48–49 [translation modified])

Some things in translating surrealism are fun; like trying to play the writer's variety of word games (or love games if we follow Breton: the words are no longer playing; they are making love). Robert Desnos is a wonderful example of this, with his parody of the Lord's Prayer, "Hour farther":

Notre paire quiète, ô yeux!
que votre "non" soit sang (t'fier?)
que votre araignée rie,
que votre vol honteux soit fête (au fait)
sur la terre (commotion).

Here is Martin Sorrell's rendering:

Hour farther witch art in Heaven
Hallowed bee, thine aim
Thy king done come!
Thy will be done in
Ersatz is in Heaven.
(Desnos 42–43)

Less comic, rarely hilarious like Desnos wordplay, Bretonian play is simpler to translate, which might seem odd, because his serious texts are far harder. But they are subject to rethinking, reviewing. Ofttimes, the slippages between the original and our work on it, or then our retranslations, can form a salute to new clearings, based on the surrealist "state of readiness," or "état d'attente," in which texts and persons are always open to new possibilities.

It is, frequently, about seeing how the entrance to the text works, as it is all-important. In the Breton poem "On me dit que là-bas," the feeling of distance is created doubly at the outset, where someone else has told the narrator about a mysterious place, situated far off, "là-bas," a beach somewhere else.

On me dit que là-bas les plages sont noires
De la lave allée à la mer
Et se déroulent au pied d'un immense pic fumant de neige
Sous un second soleil de serins sauvages
Quel est donc ce pays lointain
Qui semble tirer toute sa lumière de ta vie
Il tremble bien réel à la pointe de tes cils
Doux à ta carnation comme un linge immatériel
Frais sorti de la malle entrouverte des âges
Derrière toi
Lançant ses derniers feux sombres entre tes jambes
Le sol du paradis perdu
Glace de ténèbres miroir d'amour
Et plus bas vers tes bras qui s'ouvrent
A la preuve par le printemps
D'A P R È S
De l'inexistence du mal
Tout le pommier en fleur de la mer

They tell me that over there the beaches are black
With the lava run off to the sea
Stretched out at the foot of a great peak smoking with snow
Under a second sun of wild canaries
So what is then this far-off land
Seeming to take its light from your life
It trembles very real at the tip of your lashes
Sweet to your carnation like an intangible linen
Freshly pulled from the half-open trunk of the ages
Behind you
Casting its last somber fires between your legs
The earth of the lost paradise
Glass of shadows mirror of love
And lower towards your arms opening

On the proof by springtime
OF AFTERWARDS
Of evil's not existing
All the flowering apple tree of the sea
(*Poems* 155–56 [translation modified])

One of the multiple challenges in translating this poem is to retain the hiss of the "sous un second soleil de serins sauvages." Another is to stress the horizontal and vertical reversals—verbal, visual, and conceptual: "Et plus bas vers tes bras . . ." What is probably lost in translation is the play on evil: the "malle," or trunk, and the "mal" of evil presume the "mâle," or male, way of looking at the universe, warlike and rational, to which Breton will always oppose the feminine irrational principle, and the image of the child-woman and the mermaid, Mélusine. On the other hand, the mirroring of the glass (*glace*) and the mirror (*miroir*) can be kept, so that the reversals in the visual realm can be justified, and, finally, the reversal of fate, against the forbidden apple and the expulsion from paradise. This is a paradisiacal poem. The overturn of the unmysterious, the near-at-hand, by the marvelous, the convergence of tree and water, leads to the final denial of condemnation, through the apple tree's flowering. No more bad apples. The sun welcomes the simultaneity, at the grand traversal of frontiers, as all elements join.

My own obsession in translating Breton has to do with what I call his totalizing figures, like this apple tree of the sea, arising as they do at the very completion of the poem. Just so, the entire crossing between land and sea ends in an internal rhyme, "tree . . . sea," to stress the new opening out into a surrealizing possibility of universal change. The same kind of poetic merge takes place at the ending of "Sur la route de San Romano," where opposite elements cross into each other:

Flamme d'eau guide-moi jusqu'à la mer de feu

 ès

Flame of water lead me to the sea of fire
(*Poems* 113)

Here again the internal rhyme of the English words "lead . . . sea" ties up the conclusion—such is the occasional luck of the translator, coming across this possibility, like that of the tree and the sea.

Finally, here is Breton in his *Mad Love*, stretching out before us not just one, but a whole circus of possibilities—we have to have the courage of our convictions to enter:

> Here it is hard to tell if it is for entering or for leaving that the door of the circus of mists opens so often. The immense tent is marvelously patched by daylight. So it is easy to establish a perfect continuity between what is opened and what is veiled. It is no different in the kind of love where desire carried to the extreme appears to bloom just in order to sweep its lighthouse beam over the always new clearings of life. No depression follows upon joy. The room filled with swansdown which we were just now crossing, and which we will cross again, communicates effortlessly with nature. Speckling with blue and gold the reefs of honey devoid of any living being, I see a thousand eyes of children watching the summit that we will not be able to reach. It must be about time to set up the trapeze. (93)

Right now, hanging somewhat perilously from that trapeze of translation and retranslation, we might perceive these slipups and slippages as fruitful. It must be about time to invite the salmon and a parrot or so back in—having become "bold birds"—to make their peace. And then, or now, each of us as readers and translators might say, surprised as we are:

> I touch nothing but the heart of things I hold the thread

Bibliography

THE SALMON AND SOME PARROTS

Barnes, Julian. *Flaubert's Parrot*. London: Picador, 1985.

Boehrer, Bruce Thomas. *Parrot Culture: Our 2500-Year-Long Fascination with the World's Most Talkative Bird*. Philadelphia: University of Pennsylvania Press, 2004.

Caws, Mary Ann. "Looking: Literature's Other." *PMLA* 119 (October 2004): 1293–314.

Dawkins, Marian Stamp. *Through Our Eyes Only? The Search for Animal Consciousness*. Oxford: Oxford University Press, 1998.

Foer, Jonathan Safran. "Finitude: Selections from the Permanent Collection." *Conjunctions* 34 (Spring 2000): 73.

Grandin, Temple, and Catherine Johnson. *Animals in Translation: Using the Mysteries of Autism to Decode Animal Behavior*. New York: Scribner's, 2005.

Kamber, Gerald. *Max Jacob and the Poetics of Cubism*. Baltimore: Johns Hopkins University Press, 1971.

Pepperberg, Irene Maxine. *The Alex Studies: Cognitive and Communicative Abilities of Grey Parrots*. Cambridge, MA: Harvard University Press, 2000.

———. "Cognition in the African Grey Parrot." *Animal Learning and Behavior* 11 (1983): 179–85.

———. "Mirror Use by African Grey Parrots." *Journal of Comparative Psychology* (June 1995): 182–95.

Schwartz, Hillel. *The Culture of the Copy: Striking Likenesses, Unreasonable Facsimiles.* New York: Zone Books, 1996.

Steiner, George. *After Babel: Aspects of Language and Translation.* Oxford: Oxford University Press, 1975.

TRANSLATING TOGETHER

Mallarmé, Stéphane. *Mallarmé in Prose.* Edited by Mary Ann Caws. New York: New Directions, 2001.

GREETING, SLIPPAGE, AND SHAPING

Apollinaire, Guillaume. *Selected Writings of Guillaume Apollinaire.* Translated by Roger Shattuck. New York: New Directions, 1971.

Baudelaire, Charles. *Les Fleurs du mal.* Translated by Richard Howard. Boston: Godine, 1983.

Caws, Mary Ann, and Hermine Riffaterre. *The Prose Poem in France: Theory and Practice.* New York: Columbia University Press, 1983.

Char, René. *Poems of René Char.* Translated and edited by Mary Ann Caws and Jonathan Griffin. Princeton, NJ: Princeton University Press, 1976.

———. *Selected Poems.* Edited by Mary Ann Caws and Tina Jolas. New York: New Directions, 1992.

Derrida, Jacques. *La Contre-allée: Dérive, arrivée, catastrophe.* With Catherine Malabou. Paris: La Quinzaine littéraire (Coll. Voyager Avec . . .), 1998.

Des Forêts, Louis-René. *Ostinato.* Translated with a preface by Mary Ann Caws. Lincoln: University of Nebraska Press, 2003.

García Lorca, Federico. *The Selected Poems of Federico García Lorca.* New York: New Directions, 1955.

Gass, William H. *Reading Rilke: Reflections on the Problems of Translation.* New York: Knopf, 1999.

Góngora, Luis de. "Mientras por competir con tu cabello." In *Penguin Book of Spanish Poetry,* edited by J. M. Cohen, 112–13. Harmondsworth, UK: Penguin, 1956.

Gryphius, Andreas. "An sich Selbst." In *The Baroque Poem,* edited by Harold B. Segel, 252–53. New York: Dutton, 1974.

Hofmannsthal, Hugo von. "Unendliche Zeit." In *An Anthology of German Poetry from Hölderlin to Rilke,* edited by Angel Flores, 333–34. New York: Anchor Books, 1960.

Hugo, Victor. "Demain, dès l'aube." In *A Survey of French Literature.* Vol. 2, edited by Morris Bishop, 51. New York: Harcourt Brace, 1965.

Miller, J. Hillis. In "The Legacy of Jacques Derrida: Forum." *PMLA* 120 (March 2005): 482–84.

Mitchell, W. J. T. *What Do Pictures Want? The Lives and Loves of Images.* Chicago: University of Chicago Press, 2005.

Reverdy, Pierre. *Selected Poems.* Translated by John Ashbery, Mary Ann Caws, and Patricia Terry. Winston-Salem, NC: Wake Forest University Press, 1991.

Rilke, Rainer Maria. *Selected Poetry.* Edited and translated by Stephen Mitchell. New York: Vintage, 1982.

Ronell, Avital. In "The Legacy of Jacques Derrida: Forum." *PMLA* 120 (March 2005): 488–90.

———. "On the Misery of Theory without Poetry: Heidegger's Reading of Holderlin's 'Andendenken.'" *PMLA* 120 (January 2005): 18–26.

Sponde, Jean de. *Sonnets de la mort.* In *Penguin Book of French Verse: Sixteenth to Eighteenth Centuries,* edited by Geoffrey Brereton. Harmondsworth: Penguin, 1958.

MALLARMÉ IN ENGLAND AND AT HOME

Baudelaire, Charles. *Les Fleurs du mal.* Translated by Richard Howard. Boston: Godine, 1983.

Bloom, Harold, Paul de Man, Jacques Derrida, Geoffery Hartman, and J. Hillis Miller. *Deconstruction and Criticism.* New York: Seabury Press, 1979.

Bonnefoy, Yves. "Igitur and the Photographer." Part I. Translated by Mary Ann Caws in *Stéphane Mallarmé: Painter among the Poets,* 18–21. New York: Hunter College Art Galleries, 1999; Part II. Translated by Mary Ann Caws. *PMLA* 114 (May 1999): 329–45.

———. "La Poétique de Mallarmé." In *Stéphane Mallarmé: Igitur, Divagations, Un coup de dés,* 7–40. Paris: *Poésie*/Gallimard, 1976.

Bowie, Malcolm. *Mallarmé; or, The Art of Being Difficult.* Cambridge: Cambridge University Press, 1978.

———. *Proust among the Stars.* New York: Columbia University Press, 1999.

Caws, Mary Ann. *The Art of Interference.* Princeton, NJ: Princeton University Press, 1988.

———. "Beholding Nothing in Mallarmé." *LIT* 1 (1988): 99–106.

———. "Dancing with Mallarmé and Seurat (and Loie Fuller and La Goulue and Nijinsky)." In *Artistic Relations: Literature and the Visual Arts in Nineteenth-Century France,* edited by Peter Collier and Robert Lethbridge. New Haven, CT: Yale University Press, 1994.

Caws, Mary Ann, and Gerhard Joseph. "Naming and Not Naming: Tennyson and Mallarmé." *Victorian Poetry* 43, no. 1 (Spring 2005): 1–18.

Caws, Mary Ann, and Sarah Bird Wright. *Bloomsbury and France: Art and Friends*. New York: Oxford University Press, 2000.

Cohn, Robert Greer. *Toward the Poems of Mallarmé*. Berkeley: University of California Press, 1965.

——, ed. *Mallarmé in the Twentieth Century*. Madison, NJ: Fairleigh Dickinson University Press. London: Associated University Presses, 1998.

Fry, Roger. *Letters*. 2 vols. Edited by Denys Sutton. London: Chatto and Windus, 1972.

——. Letters of Roger Fry and Vanessa Bell (unpublished). Archives, Tate Britain. London.

Gitter, Elizabeth. "The Power of Woman's Hair in the Victorian Imagination." *PMLA* 99 (October 1984): 936–54.

Holden, Donald. *Whistler: Landscapes and Seascapes*. New York: Watson-Guptill Publications, 1976.

Lloyd, Rosemary. "Mallarmé and the Bounds of Translation." *Nottingham Friends Studies* 40 (2001): 14–25.

Mallarmé, Stéphane. *La Dernière Mode: Gazette du Monde et de la Famille*. Paris: Editions Ramsay, 1978.

——. *Mallarmé in Prose*. Edited by Mary Ann Caws. New York: New Directions, 2001.

——. *Mallarmé-Whistler Correspondance*. Recueillie, classée et annotée par C. P. Barbier. Paris: A.G. Nizet, 1964.

——. *Oeuvres complètes*. 2 vols. Edited by Bertrand Marchal. Paris: Gallimard/Pléiade, 1998.

——. *Oeuvres complètes*. Edited by Henri Mondor and G. Jean-Aubry. Paris: Gallimard/Pléiade, 1945.

——. *Poems*. Translated by Roger Fry and Charles Mauron. London: Hogarth Press, 1936.

——. *Selected Letters of Stéphane Mallarmé*. Edited and translated by Rosemary Lloyd. Chicago: University of Chicago Press, 1988.

——. *Selected Poetry and Prose*. Edited by Mary Ann Caws. New York: New Directions, 1983.

Mauron, Charles. *Des métaphores obsédantes au mythe personnel: Introduction à la psychocritique*. Paris: Libraire J. Corti, 1963.

——. *Poèmes Français et Provençaux: Evocations*. Saint-Rémy-de-Provence: n.p., 2004.

Mehlman, Jeffrey. "Mallarmé and 'Seduction Theory.' " *Paragraph* 14 (1991): 95–109.

Riffaterre, Michael. "On the Prose Poem's Formal Features." In *The Prose*

Poem in France: Theory and Practice, edited by Mary Ann Caws and Hermine Riffaterre, 117–34. New York: Columbia University Press, 1983.

Steinmetz, Jean-Luc. *Mallarmé au jour le jour*. Paris: Arthème Fayard, 1998.

Tennyson, Alfred Lord. *Poems of Tennyson*. Edited by Christopher Ricks. Berkeley: University of California Press, 1987.

Terry, Patricia. "Mallarmé and Bashô." In *Mallarmé in the Twentieth Century*, edited by Robert Greer Cohn. Madison, NJ: Fairleigh Dickinson University Press, 1998.

Valéry, Paul. *Poésies*. Paris: Gallimard, 1976.

Whistler, James Abbott McNeill. *The Gentle Art of Making Enemies*. Introduction by Alfred Werner. New York: Dover, 1967.

———. *Ten O'Clock*. Translated by Stéphane Mallarmé. Preface by Henry de Paysac. Paris: L'Echoppe, 1992.

———. *Whistler on Art: Selected Letters and Writings of James McNeill Whistler*. Edited by Nigel Thorp. Washington, DC: Smithsonian Institution Press, 1994.

Woolf, Virginia. *Moments of Being: Unpublished Autobiographical Writings*. Edited Jeanne Schulkind. New York: Harvest, 1976.

———. *Reading Notebooks*. Edited by Brenda Silver. Princeton, NJ: Princeton University Press, 1983.

WOOLF IN TRANSLATION

Caws, Mary Ann, and Nicola Luckhurst, eds. *The Reception of Virginia Woolf in Europe*. London: Continuum, 2002.

Caws, Mary Ann, and Sarah Bird Wright. *Bloomsbury and France: Art and Friends*. New York: Oxford University Press, 2000.

Hopkins, Gerard Manley. *Poems and Prose*. Harmondsworth, UK: Penguin, 1953.

Ponge, Francis. "A New Introduction to the Pebble." In *Things*. Translated by Cid Corman, 44–46. New York: Grossman, 1971.

Woolf, Virginia . *The Complete Shorter Fiction of Virginia Woolf*. Edited by Susan Dick. New York: Harcourt Brace Jovanovich, 1989.

———. "La Dame au miroir." In *Kew Gardens* (bilingual edition). Translated by Pierre Nordon, 166–77. Paris: Livre de Poche, 1993.

———. "La Dame au miroir." In *La Mort de la phalène: Nouvelles*. Translated by Hélène Bokanowski, 197–203. Paris: Seuil (Points), 1968.

———. "La Fascination de l'étang." In *La Fascination de l'étang: Proses*. Edited by Susan Dick, translated by Josée Kamoun, 152–59. Paris: Seuil, 1990.

———. "La Marque sur le mur." In *Kew Gardens* (bilingual edition). Translated by Pierre Nordon, 12–37. Paris: Livre de Poche, 1993.

———. "La Marque sur le mur." In *La Mort de la phalène: Nouvelles*. Translated by Hélène Bokanowski, 66–76. Paris: Seuil (Points), 1968.

———. "Objets massifs." In *La Mort de la phalène: Nouvelles*. Translated by Hélène Bokanowski, 77–84. Paris: Seuil (Points), 1968.

———. "Objets tangibles." In *Kew Gardens* (bilingual edition). Translated by Pierre Nordon, 62–81. Paris: Livre de Poche, 1993.

———. *Orlando*. Translated by Charles Mauron. In *Virginia Woolf: Oeuvre romanesque*, vol. 2. Paris: Stock, 1974.

———. *Orlando*. Translated by Catherine Pappo-Musard. Paris: Livre de Poche, 1993.

———. *Orlando: A Biography*. New York: Signet, 1960.

———. "La Robe Neuve." In *La Mort de la phalène: Nouvelles*. Translated Hélène Bokanowski, 165–74. Paris: Seuil (Points), 1968.

———. *Romans et nouvelles*. Translated by Pierre Nordon. Paris: Livre de Poche, 1993.

———. *A Room of One's Own*. New York: Harcourt Brace Jovanovich, 1957.

———. *A Sketch of the Past*. In *Moments of Being: Unpublished Autobiographical Writings*. Edited by Jeanne Schulkind, 64–137. New York: Harvest, 1976.

———. *Three Guineas*. New York: Harcourt Brace Jovanovich, 1966.

———. *Trois Guinées*. Translated by Viviane Forrester. Paris: des Femmes, 1977.

———. *Une chambre à soi*. Translated by Clara Malraux. Paris: Robert Marin, 1951.

———. *Les Vagues*. Translated by Cécile Wajsbrot. Paris: Calmann-Lévy, 1993.

———. *Les Vagues*. Translated by Marguerite Yourcenar. In *Oeuvre romanesque*, vol. 2. Paris: Stock, 1954.

———. *The Waves*. New York: Harcourt Brace, 1978.

POUND AT LIBERTY

Hopkins, Gerard Manley. *Poems and Prose*. Edited by W. H. Gardner. Harmondsworth, UK: Penguin, 1953.

Pound, Ezra. *Ezra Pound: Translations*. New York: New Directions, 1963.

Rimbaud, Arthur. *Oeuvres*. Edited by Suzanne Bernard. Paris: Garnier, 1960.

White, Sarah. "Lives and Reasons: A Memoir of Far Love." Unpublished ms.

BECKETT'S BUSINESS

Beckett, Samuel. *Collected Poems in English and French*. London: John Calder, 1977.

————. *Disjecta: Miscellaneous Writings and a Dramatic Fragment*. Edited by Ruby Cohn. New York: Grove Press, 1984.

Char, René. *Selected Poems*. Edited by Mary Ann Caws and Tina Jolas. New York: New Directions, 1992.

Derrida, Jacques. *The Truth in Painting*. Translated by Geoff Bennington and Ian McLeod. Chicago: University of Chicago Press, 1987.

Éluard, Paul. *Selected Writings*. Translated by Lloyd Alexander. New York: New Directions, 1951.

Kenner, Hugh. *A Reader's Guide to Samuel Beckett*. Syracuse, NY: Syracuse University Press, 1973.

————. *Samuel Beckett: A Critical Study*. London: John Calder, 1961.

Schapiro, Meyer. *Theory and Philosophy of Art: Style, Artist, and Society.* New York: Braziller, 1994.

SHAKESPEARE, KEATS, AND YEATS, BY BONNEFOY

Bonnefoy, Yves. "Douze sonnets de Shakespeare." *Nu(e)*, no. 25, special issue "Michel Collot" (March 2003): 95–106.

————. *Keats et Leopardi: Quelques traductions nouvelles*. Paris: Mercure de France, 2000.

————. *Shakespeare and the French Poet*. Edited by John Naughton. Chicago: Chicago University Press, 2004.

————. *Shakespeare et Yeats*. Paris: Mercure de France, 1998.

————. "La traduction des sonnets de Shakespeare." *Shakespeare et la France*. Société française Shakespeare, Actes du Congrès de 2000. Textes réunis et présentés par Patricia Dorval. Publiés sous la direction de Jean-Marie Maguin. Paris: Société Française Shakespeare, 2001.

Shakespeare, William. *Les Poèmes de Shakespeare, précédé de traduire en vers ou en prose*. Translated by Yves Bonnefoy. Paris: Mercure de France, 1993.

————. *Sonnets: Version française de Pierre-Jean Jouve*. Paris: Poésie/ Gallimard, 1969.

Yeats, William Butler. *Quarante-cinq poèmes de Yeats, suivis de La Résurrection*. Translated by Yves Bonnefoy. Paris: Hermann, 1989 (coll. *Poésie*/Gallimard, 1993).

CODA

Breton, André. *Communicating Vessels*. Translated by Mary Ann Caws and Geoffrey Harris. Lincoln: University of Nebraska Press, 1990.

————. *Mad Love.* Translated by Mary Ann Caws. Lincoln: University of Nebraska Press, 1987.

————. *Selected Poems.* Edited and translated by Jean-Pierre Cauvin and Mary Ann Caws. Austin: University of Texas Press, 1983.

Caws, Mary Ann, ed. and trans. *Surrealist Love Poems.* London: Tate, 2001; Chicago: University of Chicago Press, 2002.

————, ed. *Yale Anthology of Twentieth-Century French Poetry.* New Haven, CT: Yale University Press, 2004.

Desnos, Robert. "Notre Paire." Translated as "Hour farther." In *Modern French Poetry*, selected and translated by Martin Sorrell, 43. London: Forest Books, 1982.

Graham, Joseph, ed. *Difference in Translation.* Ithaca, NY: Cornell University Press, 1985.

Johnson, Barbara. "Taking Translation Philosophically." In *Difference in Translation*, edited by Joseph Graham. Ithaca, NY: Cornell University Press, 1985.

Index of Names